ESSE

ECONOMICS

FOR NON-ECONOMISTS

CHARVI SHUKLA

notionpress
.com

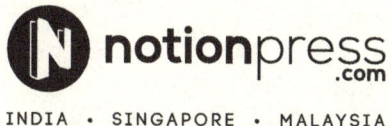

INDIA • SINGAPORE • MALAYSIA

Notion Press

No.8, 3rd Cross Street,
CIT Colony, Mylapore,
Chennai, Tamil Nadu – 600004

First Published by Notion Press 2021
Copyright © Charvi Shukla 2021
All Rights Reserved.

ISBN 978-1-63714-730-6

This book has been published with all efforts taken to make the material error-free after the consent of the author. However, the author and the publisher do not assume and hereby disclaim any liability to any party for any loss, damage, or disruption caused by errors or omissions, whether such errors or omissions result from negligence, accident, or any other cause.

While every effort has been made to avoid any mistake or omission, this publication is being sold on the condition and understanding that neither the author nor the publishers or printers would be liable in any manner to any person by reason of any mistake or omission in this publication or for any action taken or omitted to be taken or advice rendered or accepted on the basis of this work. For any defect in printing or binding the publishers will be liable only to replace the defective copy by another copy of this work then available.

To my family – Mom, Dad, Atharva
My friends – Anandi, Sia

CONTENTS

Foreword   7

Chapter 1 Scarcity and Choice   11
    Resources   12
    Market Structures   14
    Important Economic Concepts   15

Chapter 2 Law of Demand and Supply   21
    Law of Demand   21
    Factors Causing Shifts in the Demand Curve   23
    Law of Supply   25
    Factors Influencing Supply   26
    Price Elasticity   27

Chapter 3 Classifying Organizations   35
    1. Sole Proprietorship   36
    2. Partnership   37
    3. Private Limited Company   39
    4. Public Limited Company   40
    5. Multinational Corporation (MNC)   42
    6. Co-operatives   44
    Types of Market Structures   45

Contents

Chapter 4 Utility Theory and Indifference Curves — 57
- Marginal Rate of Substitution — 59
- The Equi-Marginal Principle — 60
- Income and Substitution Effect — 61
- Costs and Revenue — 63
- Relationship Between Marginal Cost and Marginal Product — 66

Chapter 5 Government's Microeconomic Intervention — 69
- Efficiency — 70
- Taxation — 74
- Tax Rates and Different Taxation Systems — 79
- Subsidies — 82

Chapter 6 Macroeconomics — 87
- Aggregate Demand — 88
- Aggregate Supply — 89
- Keynesian vs Monetarist Views — 90
- Inflation — 91
- Gross Domestic Product — 93
- Economic Growth — 94
- Measuring GDP — 97
- Unemployment — 100

Chapter 7 Countercyclical Economic Policies — 109
- Monetary Policy — 109
- Fiscal Policy — 110
- Supply Side Policies — 112
- Nationalization vs. Privatization — 113

Epilogue — *115*

FOREWORD

When I started to learn economics, I would always get scared thinking that it is complicated and requires mugging up definitions. I always struggled with understanding the business sections of newspapers and magazines. Then, in the summer of 2019, I got the opportunity to take the Harvard summer course in Principles of Economics. It was taught by Professor Daron Acemoglu from MIT, Professor John A-List from the University of Chicago, and Professor David Laibson from Harvard University. They explained ideas in a simple, straightforward, and intuitive manner. That is from where I got the inspiration to write this book. Economics must be made accessible to everyone and the only way to do that is to make it less daunting, as some may call it.

Economics is not some sort of a complex evil monstrosity with Multivariable Calculus being the only tool that makes it useful in real-life scenarios. Economics is essentially based on reasoning and logic. Simply put, economics is a social science that studies how people interact with things of value. There are multiple economic agents who interact and try to optimize. They are basically doing what's best for them–being logical. All the other complicated concepts of economics stem from logic. Logic defines strict principles of validity in terms of rules. These rules can be enumerated in the "language of logic." The syllogism, "If it's sunny, I'll go to the mall. It's sunny. I'll go to the mall," can be formalized as the rule "If P implied Q, and Q holds, then P holds."

This means that if one is able to reason with an open and free mentality, understanding economics would become incredibly easy. That is the aim of this book. To help you reason economically. To help these basic concepts sink in. Any other concept can be built on top of this.

Starting from the core of scarcity and choice, we would go on to understand the laws of demand and supply. From here, different market structures and types of firms would be analyzed. These can then be observed in real-life scenarios. For instance, one would be able to realize how a "*sabzi mandi*" is a close example of a perfectly competitive market while the toothpaste industry is an oligopoly. To make matters more interesting, a little bit of game theory (and, obviously, prisoner's dilemma) is included in the book. After learning about the producer's viewpoint of economics, the consumer's perspective is understood in the Utility and Choice Theory. This is the part where economics is about *you*.

The macroeconomic theory section is what will help you understand the "business" section of a newspaper. Once you know about countercyclical policies and the RBI's interest rates, you would actually be able to make sense out of what Nirmala Sitharaman and Shashikanata Das are doing up there.

It is important to never be daunted by the mere idea of something. Once you try it out, you will be free to make opinions about it. Try out economics.

Chapter-1
SCARCITY

Chapter 1

SCARCITY AND CHOICE

Imagine having an incredibly large sum of money. So much money that it's pretty much impossible to run out. Now take a piece of paper and write down all that you would like to purchase. A video game, some clothes, a new television, a mobile phone. But the money is unlimited, right? So, you would want to buy larger and more expensive things such as cars, houses, tennis courts, malls, and on and on!

You will notice that no matter how modest you are your wants are unlimited. However, in real-life scenarios, everyone doesn't have insane amounts of money. This is how the concepts of scarcity and choice originate. You have unlimited wants but only a limited amount of resources (that is money in the above example), which is why you experience a "scarcity" of resources to fulfill all of your wants. This concept is very important in economics because it can be applied almost everywhere. For instance, a businessman has a limited amount of land to build a factory on, a government has limited money to spend on its country's citizens, a student has limited time to prepare for an exam, etc.

Scarcity is why you have to make choices in day-to-day life. Say, Jessi has a 20-dollar bill. She has to make a choice about how she is going to spend it. She can buy a $20-book or a $20-t-shirt. However, it is important to note that she cannot get both things because she only has $20. but together they cost $40. Hence, she has to make a choice about what she wants. At this point, you must be thinking pfft! Isn't this common sense? Why would this be a "pillar" of economics? Well, the concept of choice and scarcity is what drives the behavior of many economic agents. From an ordinary girl like Jessi to Jeff Bezos, all experience choice and scarcity. Scarcity is what, as you will find later, leads to the formation of price mechanism and competition in a market.

Resources

Resources are used up during the production process. It is a process that converts input into output. Resources, or factors of production, act as inputs and can be categorized into four types, namely land, labor, capital, and enterprise. All of these resources are necessary for a business to start and function properly.

1.1 Land

Land includes any natural resource used for producing goods or services. This does not necessarily have to be a flat patch of land. The wilderness, minerals, flora and fauna are also included in the factor of "land." For instance, if someone owns 10 hectares of land and the land contains oil, technically, the person owns the oil too. This is one of the major reasons for different land prices around the world. Land is important to a business because there needs to be space to conduct

office work or build a factory. Interestingly, the advent of the gig economy (people who work for Uber or Zomato) and development of technology has made land less important, as people can do some types of work from anywhere at any time. Rent is earned on land.

1.2 Labor

Labor is the human effort put into the production process. It is generally further categorized into white collar and blue collar labor. Blue collar labor refers to the typical manual labor. This may be observed in farms, construction sites, and textile mills where people require physical strength and energy. On the other hand, white collar jobs include professional office work carried out by accountants, consultants, etc. These jobs have more to do with knowledge in contrast to strength. Wages are earned by workers on hourly or daily basis and salaries are earned on a monthly basis.

1.3 Capital

Capital is any manmade resource that acts as an asset to a firm. This includes machinery, equipment, and raw materials. Money has to be put in to purchase these capital goods. This spending of money on capital to produce goods in the future is called investment. With time, some machines and equipment wear out or depreciate and have to be replaced from time to time. Gross investment is given by

total investment minus net depreciation. Interest is the return for investment.

Another kind of capital is called "human capital." It has become particularly important in recent years for development in information technology (IT) and artificial intelligence (AI) fields. It refers to the skillsets and knowledge possessed by a worker. Higher human capital leads to higher productivity-higher output per worker hour. Education is important, so focus!

1.4 Enterprise

Enterprise is the risk-bearing factor of production. It is the person who takes the initiative to bring together all other factors and economic agents for a business to function. The entrepreneur takes the financial risk and incurs losses if the business fails and enjoys profits if succeeds.

It is essential that a firm has access to all four factors of production. Although, labor and capital can be substituted for each other depending on the kind of work taken up by the firm. For example, a silicon chip industry is more capital intensive and the sales industry is more labor-intensive. Quantity of factors of production required varies but all of them are still necessary.

Market Structures

In economics, firms can be primary, secondary, or tertiary sector. Each of these has specific qualities that differentiate them from the other. The primary sector deals with the extraction of raw materials. This can include mining, fishing, farming, and horticulture. Most of the work in this sector is labor-intensive. The secondary sector deals with manufacturing finished products from raw materials. Value is added to the raw materials as they get processed, leading to higher prices of finished goods. A finished cotton dress is more expensive than a bag full of cotton that was used to make the dress. Secondary sector includes industries such as textiles, automobiles, etc. Tertiary sector includes services and not finished goods. Doctors, accountants, psychologists are all a part of the tertiary sector. A newly emerging sector is the quaternary sector and is considered as a sub part of the tertiary sector by some. It is the knowledge-based sector of the economy and deals with research and development of new technologies, media, information sector, and more.

When countries grow and develop into more economically developed countries, they transition from primary to secondary to finally tertiary sector economies. This trend can be seen in more developed countries such as the United States. Less developed countries like Nigeria have economies that are majorly dependent on their primary sector (agriculture and mining-based industries). Interestingly, India has shown an anomalous growth pattern. It has transitioned directly from a primary agriculture-based economy to a fast-growing tertiary sector-based economy.

Important Economic Concepts

Optimization

Consider this situation: you have an important economics exam tomorrow. You can either watch Netflix or revise a few economic concepts. What will you do? Correct, revising will enable you to remember concepts and score higher on the exam. This is why it is the "optimum choice." Now let's go back to Jessi. She can go to shop A and get a pair of socks for $4 or she can go to shop B and get three pairs of socks for $9. Going to shop B is the optimum choice because she would be paying less per pair of socks, meaning she is maximizing her profits. The assumption made here is that Jessi has complete information about sock prices in each of the two firms and is rational enough to purchase the cheaper socks over the more expensive ones. Therefore, the optimal choice is the one where a consumer makes the most feasible choice with the given information and assuming that the consumer is rational.

Opportunity Cost

Opportunity cost is defined as the cost of the next best opportunity forgone when a choice is made. For instance, when a student had to decide which AP class she wanted to take in school, she narrowed it down to either Mathematics or Physics. She cannot take both classes because her schedule does not allow it. The student ended up choosing to take AP Physics and so the opportunity cost of her choice would be learning AP Mathematics. The opportunity cost of government spending on education is government spending on infrastructure or unemployment benefits. For Jessi, the opportunity cost of buying socks from shop B is to buy socks from shop A. In layman's language, it is the cost you would have paid if you had chosen what you did not choose.

Positive vs. Normative Economic Statements

Positive economic statements are objective and are based on empirical evidence. They describe what people normally and actually do. Normative economic statements are subjective and are based on value judgments. They recommend what people ought to do.

"The US government spends $12,500 on average per student in a public school," is a positive statement. While "Governments should pay more attention to problems faced by pregnant women in the workforce," is a normative statement.

Positive statements are used when an idea needs to be illustrated or a point needs to be proven. Conversely, a normative statement is required when suggestions and speculations are being made.

Chapter - 2

LAW OF DEMAND AND SUPPLY

Chapter 2

LAW OF DEMAND AND SUPPLY

Law of Demand

Jessi's mother gives her pocket money every month. Jessi loves to eat ice cream and spends most of her pocket money on ice cream. Last month, each ice cream used to cost $4, which meant that she bought 2 ice creams. But this month, the ice cream parlor is having a sale and each ice cream costs only $3 now. This means that she will purchase three ice creams this time (and hopefully not get diabetes). A couple of months later, she goes on vacation and finds a fancy ice cream shop that sells one ice cream for $6! She says, "Wait, this is crazy. I'm not going to waste money like that!" And so, she doesn't get any.

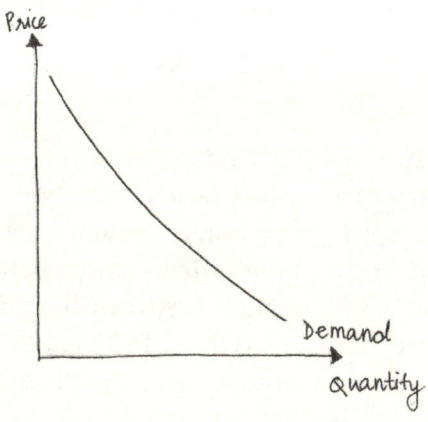

If we list down the different prices and the corresponding quantities of ice cream that she buys, we will discover an inverse relationship between price and quantity. This is because when products are more expensive, either people are not willing to pay such a high price or they don't have the amount of money required to purchase the product. It is important to note that the "want" and "demand" are not the same, and therefore, must not be confused. Demand can be defined as the willingness and ability of a person to purchase a product. Whereas wants can be of anything and whether or not one can afford the product is irrelevant. I can sit in my house wanting a Tesla, but that will not be counted as demand for a Tesla because I cannot afford it.

A table containing price and quantity demanded is called a demand schedule. A demand curve is obtained when price is plotted on the y-axis and quantity demanded is plotted on the x-axis. It is a pictorial representation of the law of demand.

Price	Quantity
3	3
4	2
6	0

Broadly, It Is Dependent on Three Factors:

1. Price of the product (how expensive is the product?)

2. Income and budget of the consumer (do I have the money to bear the expense?)

3. Tastes and preferences of the consumer (do I want the product?)

Law of Demand states that all other things being constant, the price of a product varies inversely with demand for the product. It depicts the natural consumer behavior and is derived from the law of diminishing marginal utility, which we will discuss later. This implies that when the price of a product decreases, there is an expansion in quantity demanded and when the price of the product increases, there is a contraction in quantity demanded. It is shown graphically as movements of points along the curve

However, when other factors are considered, there may be instances when demand for a product is higher or lower at each and every price. This is known as increase or decrease in demand. It reflects as shifts in the demand curve.

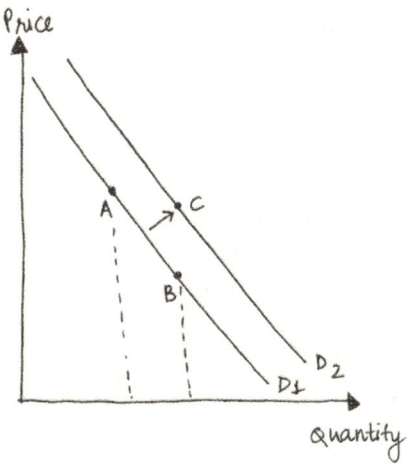

Factors Causing Shifts in the Demand Curve

1. Income

Naturally, when you have more money you will demand more goods at each and every price. This causes a rightward shift in the demand curve. Similarly, when income is less, spending decreases at every price. Two types of goods include normal goods and inferior goods. They behave differently with changes in income. Normal goods (act normally) are subjected to a higher demand when incomes rise. Hence, the demand for normal goods is directly proportional to demand. On the other hand, inferior goods, as the name suggests, are of comparatively poor quality. Hence, when people get more money, they switch from such goods to better quality goods. For instance, the demand for a Nokia phone will decrease if people have higher incomes. More and more people will substitute Nokia phones for Apple iPhones or Samsung phones. This means that the demand for inferior goods is inversely related to incomes earned by people.

2. Availability of Related Goods

Complementary Goods

If you go to the supermarket, you get coffee and sugar together. To use coffee, you must have sugar. Therefore, they are complementary goods and the price of one will influence the demand for another. For instance, the sugar farmers in your locality had a production boom and so sugar is cheaper now. Since you'll have a higher demand for sugar, your demand for coffee will be higher (you will need more coffee to use all of the sugar). As you can see, the price of the goods we care about is inversely proportional to the price of the complementary goods. If the price of sugar were to rise, the demand for coffee will decrease!

Substitute Goods

Substitute goods, as the name suggests, are two goods that can be used in place of one another. Coca-Cola and Pepsi, coffee and tea, milk powder and milk are a few examples.

Now question yourself. What will happen if Coca-Cola becomes cheaper? Will you still purchase Pepsi? The simple law of demand logic says no. You will substitute Pepsi for Coca-Cola because you think that they are similar and can be substituted. Hence, a fall in the price of Coca-Cola causes a fall in demand for Pepsi. The price and quantity of both move in the same direction.

3. Taxation

Taxes are mandatory payments made to the government. The difference between income and amount paid in tax is called disposable income. This income can be spent on goods and services. When the Fed increases the tax rates, consumers are left with less money to spend. This means that they will purchase less goods and services.

4. Advertisements

Advertisements are all a game of psychology and shape the perceptions of millions of people that watch them. You start feeling that using Pepsodent will make your teeth 99.99% germ-free while you still face the risk of getting cavities. Companies hire renowned actors and good cinematographers who try to create brand loyalty and persuade the consumption of a given product. If an advertising campaign is successful, more people will purchase the goods, and hence, the demand for the product at every price will be higher.

Law of Supply

Now think of yourself as a greedy businessman who produces sports shoes. If the market price for sports shoes is low, you would want to supply less shoes. But when the market price is higher, you would want to sell more shoes because the total amount of money that you would earn

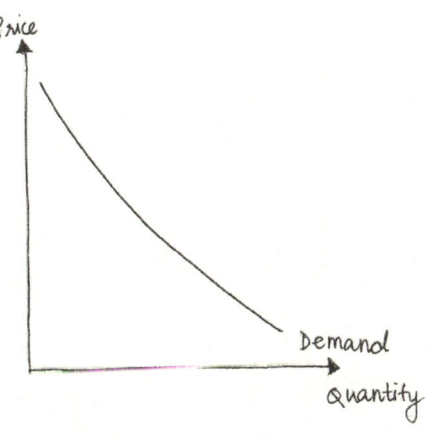

will be higher. This holds true for every producer and is called the law of supply. Supply is defined as the willingness and ability to supply a product. It must not be confused with production. Produced goods can be stored and supplied later when the producer wants to. Since any business wants to maximize profits, they sell more goods when the price is higher.

The table below shows a supply schedule, which lists the quantity supplied and the corresponding price of your shoes.

When this data is plotted on an x-y plane, a supply curve is obtained.

Price	Quantity
10	3
15	4
20	6
25	8

The law of supply states that the price of a product and the quantity supplied has an inverse relationship.

Factors Influencing Supply

1. Cost of Production

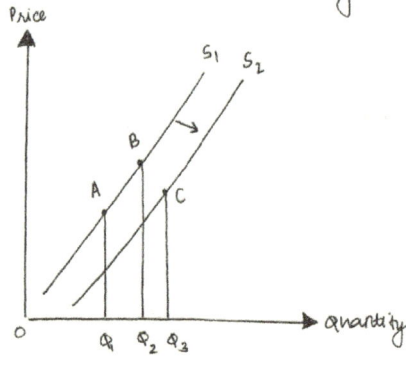

Cost of production includes the costs of all factors of production (land, labor, capital, and enterprise). When these costs are lower, firms prefer to produce more than when they are higher. Cell phones contain silicon chips. When the price of silicon, the raw material, is lower, the firm is able to produce more output and sell it at the same unit price as before. This leads to a rightward shift in the supply curve. The opposite happens when the cost of producing goods becomes higher.

2. Government Subsidies and Corporation Tax

Government subsidies are grants given by the government to businesses. In simple words, the government covers some part of your cost of producing goods. This means your cost of production is lower and you can supply more at every price. Consequently, a high corporation tax (a tax levied on businesses) leads to a higher cost of production. This means less will be supplied when taxes are too high.

3. Discovery of Resources

When more oil gets discovered, the supply of oil increases. Interestingly, this also reduces the prices of oil, causing the supply of other goods that use oil as a raw material (mostly everything) to increase. Oil can have a huge impact on a country's economy. No wonder there are price wars for oil. Just as discovery causes an increase in supply, destruction of resources causes a decrease in supply. This may result from pandemics, wars or natural disasters.

4. Size of the Market

Imagine being a firm in your locality. You supply goods only in your neighborhood and your competition is your neighbors. Now consider a situation where you've just received a call saying that you've been appointed as the new CEO of Amazon. Now you sell goods to the whole world economy. You must have noticed that the total amount of goods that you will have to supply in your locality will be much lower than what would be required by Amazon. With this example, I am trying to emphasize the importance of market size in determining the supply of a firm. The larger the market, the greater the quantity of goods supplied.

Price Elasticity

Price Elasticity of Demand

Price Elasticity of demand is defined as the degree of responsiveness of quantity demanded to a change in price. In simple language, it means by what percentage will your demand for a good change when its price changes. Price elasticity of demand, or PED, is given by percentage change in quantity demanded/percentage change in price. It is a ratio that always comes out to be negative because demand and price have an inverse relationship.

Example 1.

Price of pajamas increases from $10 to $15. This results in the quantity demanded of pajamas to decrease from 200 units to only 50 units.

Percentage change in price = 5/10 * 100

= 50%

Percentage change in quantity demanded = –150/200 * 100

= –75%

PED = –75/50

= –1.5

The negative sign can be disregarded as it only shows the relationship between quantity demanded and price. The magnitude of this figure describes how consumers will react to changes in prices. If PED>1, then demand for the given goods is said to be price elastic. This means that the percentage change in demand exceeds the percentage change in price for the product. Increasing the price of pajamas by 1% decreases the quantity demanded by 1.5%. In other words, consumers are very price-sensitive and change their spending even when there's a minimal

change in the price. Such a demand is known as elastic demand. Luxury goods such as cars, TVs and jewelry face elastic demand because their purchase can be delayed. Buying a diamond necklace is not about life and death (unless you are really spoiled).

Conversely, if this figure was smaller than 1, then the demand would have been said to be inelastic. As the name suggests, changes in price will not impel or trigger the customers to change the amount of such goods that they purchase. A large percentage change in price will have a proportionally smaller change in quantity demanded (PED would still remain negative). Such a demand is seen in essential goods where the consumption is necessary, so the price doesn't matter. For example, medical facilities, food grains, and clothes are a few examples of essential goods.

Unit elastic demand occurs when PED=1 and changes in price cause a proportional change in quantity demanded. There are other extreme elasticities of demand that do not exist in real life but are worth studying. The first one is "perfectly elastic demand." This means that PED is infinity and even if you increase the price by just one cent, the demand would change infinitely. The second one is "perfectly inelastic demand," and as the name suggests, the elasticity value is zero.

No matter how expensive the product becomes (infinite dollars theoretically), the quantity demanded would remain unchanged. It is quite difficult to find examples of such extremes in real life. For instance, very expensive ornaments, jewelry, and paintings have a perfectly elastic demand. If the price increases, people stall their purchases hoping for lower prices in the future. Similarly, important healthcare services such as bypass surgeries and cancer treatments have a perfectly inelastic demand. People are ready to pay any amount to save their lives.

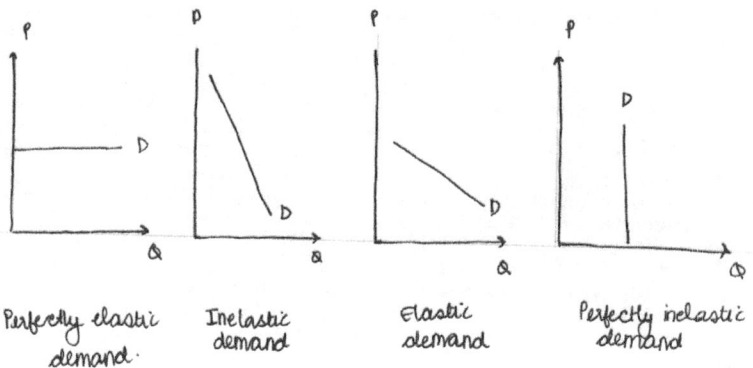

Price Elasticity of Supply

To get an intuition for the elasticity concept, the best tactic is to put yourself into the producer or the consumer's shoes. So imagine yourself as a business person who sells towels. If the market price of towels rises, then you will naturally want to supply more because that will earn you more revenue. If the price decreases, you will simply throw all the extra towels in a godown and sell them later when the price is higher. On the contrary, if you are an apple farmer, you will not be able to change the supply that easily because apples are not durable and would obviously rot in a couple of weeks.

The degree to which you alter your supply when price changes is known as the price elasticity of supply. Just like demand, there can be perfectly elastic, elastic, unit elastic, inelastic, and perfectly inelastic supply. It can be noted that PES values are always positive because of the direct relationship between price and quantity supplied. When supply is elastic, it can be "stretched" more than the stretch in price (try and compare this to an elastic band), hence, PES>1. When the supply is inelastic, the elastic band is rigid and doesn't change much with changes in price. For this reason PES<1.

In a perfectly elastic supply (PES=infinite), small changes in price can cause an infinite change in quantity. It means that one is willing to supply as many units of goods as possible at a given price. If the price increases or decreases, then the quantity would become zero. A near example of a perfectly elastic supply can be currencies. You cannot bargain your way into purchasing currency though it is sold at a higher price in black markets at times.

When any percentage change in price, no matter how large, results in zero change in quantity supplied, the given product is said to have a perfectly inelastic supply. Land, paintings from deceased artists, and the Kohinoor diamond are all priced possessions that are very limited in supply. Therefore, they have a perfectly inelastic supply. It is very intuitive because no matter how much money you pay, you cannot create land out of nowhere or original paintings by a dead person unless you have been gifted with magic!

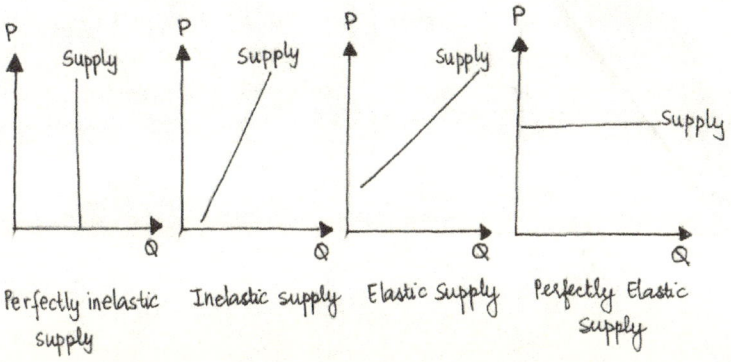

Why Learn About Price Elasticity?

At this point, you might be wondering why am I supposed to know all this economic jargon? How is it useful at all? It turns out that the concept of price elasticity is very important. Producers and businesses can work up their pricing strategies according to the price elasticity of demand. The more inelastic the demand for the goods is, the higher prices can be charged without losing a considerable amount of sales. For instance, higher prices of oil can be charged because it is required every day to run homes and many substitutes are not available. So, whatever the price may be, the consumers will have to purchase the oil.

When governments formulate their policies, they always have the idea of price elasticity of demand on their mind. A tax will be most effective in reducing the quantity demanded of a good only when the demand for that good is elastic. The increase in price due to tax will significantly decrease consumption. When items such as cigarettes and liquor are taxed, large amounts of revenue are generated because people are addicted to these goods and are ready to pay high taxes. The idea of price elasticity, as we will see later, also determines the amount of tax that producers can pass on to consumers in the form of higher prices. Similarly, a subsidy will be most beneficial when the supply of a good is elastic. The increase in price will enable the producer to increase the quantity of goods produced. If not the exact elasticity value, even a rough estimate of price elasticity can enable consumers, producers, and governments to optimize their strategies.

Chapter - 3
CLASSIFYING ORGANIZATIONS

Chapter 3

CLASSIFYING ORGANIZATIONS

A firm is a legal entity that engages in business activities to earn profits by providing professional services and products. A company contains a group of two or more people aimed at a common goal. It is essential to understand the difference between a firm and a company. A company is basically a subset of the different types of firms that exist in an economy. Hence, every company will be a firm but every firm is not a company. For example, one can have a law firm because one person owns and runs it. On the other hand, one can have a steel business or a steel company. A company requires more than one person but a firm can be a sole proprietorship.

There are multiple types of firms in the economy. They include sole proprietorship, partnership, public limited companies, private limited companies, co-operatives, multinational companies, state-owned enterprises, and unions. We will dive right into each category and discuss them in-depth.

1. Sole Proprietorship

Nero used to kill time during his summer vacation and this made his mother really mad. One evening, after getting a long lecture from his mother, he decided to start his own business. He took all of his pocket money and bought one-kilo lemons. He constructed a small stall using materials from his garage. After this was done he made a huge signboard that said "Truly Lemon Lemonade." He had started his very own lemonade business.

This kind of business that is owned and run by one person is known as a sole proprietorship. Nero, the sole proprietor, will earn all the profits and bear all the losses that the business makes. Such businesses are generally very small-scaled and are unable to grow because of the lack of investment and financial capital. No matter how rich Nero is or how much pocket money his parents give him, his business will never be able to match up to a large beverage company such as Coca-Cola. Although the owner gets to benefit from all the profits, any losses or legal bills also have to be borne by the owner. This is because, in a sole

proprietorship, the sole proprietor is an unlimited liability to his business. Any business is said to have unlimited liability when the business owners have full legal responsibility for all business debts. If under any circumstances, the owner(s) are unable to fulfill these debts, obligations are paid through seizure and sale of personal assets. In easy language, if you are a sole proprietor and you don't pay your bills, the feds will show up tomorrow morning to take away your house and all your belongings to pay the debts. Under the eyes of the law, both the firm and the owner are the same legal entity. Due to this unlimited liability, owners generally refrain from taking risks. There may also be a shortage of ideas because there is potentially just one person to think. Decision-making is faster and there are no feuds because of the single ownership of the business. It is a cycle: small business implies less profit, less profit implies less reinvestment, and hence, the firm always remains small. If the entrepreneur wants full control over the firm and wants it to remain small scale, starting a sole proprietorship is the best option for him.

2. Partnership

Nero's plan of starting the lemonade business does not work out. Barely three or four people showed up. So, Nero decided to ask two of his friends to help out in the business. Since there were three people now, they had more money to spend. All of them sat and brainstormed ideas that they could employ. In the end, they decided to buy mason jars and mint for their lemonade. This not only enhanced sales revenue but also made their product better taste-wise.

Partnerships typically have between 2 and 20 people involved. Even if one of the partners decided to quit, the partnership gets dissolved and the whole paperwork has to be done again. Just like sole proprietorships, partnerships also have unlimited liability. This can create a lot of problems for the business, as it implies that all the costs and benefits from the business will be shared between the partners and they will have to pay out of their own pockets if they are unable to pay off all liabilities. For instance, if Nero and one of his colleagues happen to disagree about something and get into a fight, the decision-making would be slow leading to inefficiencies. The business would not be able to respond to consumer preferences fast enough and would not be competitive. In the case of death, insolvency, or bankruptcy of any of the members, the business stops existing.

However, as we saw in Nero's example, a partnership can generate a larger amount of money and capital because a larger number of people can pool in a larger amount of money. There will be more innovation and human capital available. Ultimately, it is a mere idea and it is the implementation that makes a business successful. Since partnerships don't grow that large in size, the owners will be able to give personal attention to customers/clients as well as the employees. This is not possible in larger firms. In addition, a single person will not have to bear all the responsibility of the business. This would reduce stress on the owners as they will have partners who have their backs.

3. Private Limited Company

Ambitious of earning more profits and growing their firm further, Nero and his friends decide to turn "Truly Lemon Lemonade" into a private limited company. A private limited company typically contains between 2 and 200 members. A huge benefit of having a private limited company is the fact that the members have limited liability to the company. The only amount of money they have at stake is the amount of investment they made in the business. Hence, the business and the members are different legal entities under the law. These firms are medium-sized and don't need to release a prospectus (a legal disclosure document that provides information about investments). Shares of this company cannot be sold to the general public on a stock exchange. Instead, personal acquaintance is required for the sale and purchase of shares. Since there can be over a hundred owners of such a company, a board of directors have to be appointed. All others are called silent partners. The board of directors is responsible for the day-to-day management and functioning of the company. They are the "face" of the company.

Private limited companies are generally medium-sized firms and only very few become large companies. Oberoi Hotels, Marriott, and Ola are a few examples of Indian private limited companies. The benefit that Nero wants to gain from this evolution is the relatively easy access to investment, funding and capital. This would enable him to expand out of his local area into a larger, possibly national, market. He will also be relieved from bearing all risks of the company. Larger sized firms are also able to invest in advertising which creates brand loyalty. This can be a very important factor in boosting the demand for a company's products. Similarly, money can be invested in research and development. Although this would help in boosting sales only in the long run, such an investment can lead to a dramatic improvement in the quality of goods and the productivity of labor. On the flip side, such a company may be subject to feuds between owners and slow decision-making due to the size of the enterprise. The transition from a sole proprietorship or a partnership into a full-blown private limited company can substantially decrease the flexibility of the system. There is a clear trade-off between control and growth of the firm.

4. Public Limited Company

Truly Lemon Lemonade Pvt. Ltd. was a successful firm. Nero and his friends had grown their firm considerably by converting their partnership into a private limited company. However, ambitious as they were, they wanted access to an even larger market. This is when Nero's father suggested that he should get his company listed and convert it to a Public Limited Company.

A public limited company has to offer the stocks of its company to the general public. This is done by getting listed on a stock exchange. A stock exchange is a market dedicated to the purchase and sale of stocks. They provide a secure environment for trading with a large number of people, as well as liquidity in a market. Stocks are simply "units of a company's ownership," so if you purchase some stocks of Colgate, you will have fractional ownership of Colgate. People who own stocks of a company are referred to as shareholders.

To get his company on the stock exchange, Nero will have to conduct an initial public offering. During this process, the shares of Truly Lemon Lemonade Pvt. Ltd. will be available in a primary market. Here, new securities are issued and financing is done based on equity or equity-based securities. The sales of the company will, hence, have an initial beginning price for the stock market. After this is done, the shares of Truly Lemon

Lemonade Inc. can be sold on the secondary market,.i.e the stock exchange. Examples of stock exchanges include the New York Stock exchange, Bombay Stock Exchange, and Nasdaq. These exist in a physical location but these days stock exchanges exist online as well. Suppose the shares of Truly Lemon Lemonade Inc. are said to become cheaper in the future. More and more people will sell their shares now thinking that if they wait, prices will fall more and they might have to end up selling those shares for an even lower price. Such a market is called a bearish market. On the other hand, if investors feel that the prices of stocks will increase in the future, they will try to buy more of those stocks. This is called a bullish market.

There are multiple advantages to being a public limited company. Firstly, the firm is exposed to a much larger market. Being listed on the stock exchange enables firms to generate capital easily (when someone purchases shares, the company gets money). The amount of money and exposure available is substantially greater than in private companies or partnerships. In fact, companies such as Apple and Amazon are public limited companies. The larger capital enables a firm to benefit from "being large scale." Costs per unit get divided over a larger output and a firm's profit per unit increases. This profit can be reinvested in the company to improve its performance further. Research and development play a crucial role in the growth of firms. Another advantage is that the shareholders and the company are considered different legal entities. This means that shareholders, i.e. owners, have limited liability in the company. Their assets will not be seized in case the firm becomes bankrupt. Firms are supposed to publish an annual account of their business annually. This enables the "general public" that is trading on the stock market to know about the company and its profitability. Similarly, they are required to hold annual shareholder meetings where the board of directors is elected. Votes are not equal. The vote of a person owning 10% of a company is stronger than the vote of a person owning 0.5% of a company. The elected directors are the "face of the company" and manage the day-to-day functioning of the company. If a director is incompetent, he/she may be removed in the next annual shareholders' meeting.

This kind of market contains agents such as investors, traders, and brokers. Brokers are the middle people who facilitate the purchase and sale of shares. They earn a commission after a transaction is made. Investors purchase and hold shares over a long time in hope of earning profits, known as dividends, in the long run. On the contrary, traders can enter and exit the market in the short run. Once shares are made available in a stock market, a given firm does not get to decide who can purchase them. If somebody does purchase them, the owners cannot refuse. This often leads to the acquisition and mergers of firms. If someone has 51% of shares in a company, he gains majority ownership in the company and can influence the decisions made.

One disadvantage of going public is that some medium-sized companies might struggle to bear the costs associated with stock exchanges and IPO. Let's take an example. SNAP Inc., the company that made Snapchat, raised $3.4 billion in March 2017 and bullish investors bought their stocks. However, the company was unable to hold on to those gains or experience a growth in the number of users. The shareholders sued the company for providing wrong information in May. It was only in 2020 that SNAP Inc. settled.

Ultimately, trading on the stock market is all about taking risks. It may lead to phenomenal profits or all the investment might be lost if the company does not flourish.

5. Multinational Corporation (MNC)

A multinational corporation functions in more than one company. These companies not only sell their products in multiple countries but also carry out production processes abroad. However, their headquarters are situated in the home country. Such companies are generally public corporations and are huge in size. Some popular examples of multinational companies include Microsoft, Sony, Tata Motors Limited, and Pepsi Co.

They benefit from economies of scale, which allows their products to be sold at very low prices. This means that demand is high all around the world. MNCs also target to produce in countries that have low corporation tax. At times, they can completely avoid tax barriers which may be experienced when goods are exported from one country to another. Multinational companies further decrease their costs of production by using cheap labor in newly developing countries. For example, the daily wage in India is substantially lower than the daily wage in America if the amount is expressed in the same currency. Hence, goods can be produced at a low cost in India and sold at home and abroad.

Governments have varying opinions about such companies. On one hand, they provide more employment opportunities, which push more and more people out of poverty. Consumption also increases as good quality products at lower prices are available in the market. In the long run, more employment and consumption stimulate the country's economic growth. Factories and offices of an MNC also accelerate infrastructure growth in a developing economy.

On the other hand, some governments oppose MNCs by issuing high tariffs and quotas. They are concerned about the smaller native companies that would obviously be unable to compete with the ginormous multinational companies and the detrimental impact of such companies on the local environment.

In some cases, if the company provides too much employment and benefits to the economy of one country, they start to pressurize the government to behave according to their will. One historic example of a multinational company that exploited another country is the British East India Company. Their actions exploited the natives and made a lot of people fall below the poverty line. The company also had considerable control over the existing rulers of India.

6. Co-operatives

A co-operative is owned and run by its members. Unlike public companies, each person has an equal vote in decision-making and the amount of shares held is inconsequential. Co-operatives are available to everyone irrespective of the collateral that the person has to offer. This open membership leads to the democratic functioning of the financial organization. Their primary purpose is to benefit their members either by providing goods at lower prices through bulk buying or paying higher interest if the co-op is a bank. For instance, credit unions (the most popular form of co-operatives) pay higher-than-average interest rates and are only accessible to those that have accounts.

The benefits of being a co-operative are maximum when there is a large membership. As more members join, the financial co-operative has more resources to offer financial products, reduced fees, lower interest rates on loans, etc. It will be wrong to assume that co-operatives remain extremely small because their main aim is not profit maximization. One great example of a worker co-operative is the Indian Coffee House, a restaurant chain in India. It has over 400 branches all across the country and 13 co-operative societies to run the coffee houses. These societies are governed by managing committees elected from the employees.

Types of Market Structures

Earlier we discussed the types of firms that can exist in a market. Now we shall move on to discuss the different types of market structures. Market structures are essentially frameworks into which the many economic agents are manifested. These include perfect competition, monopolistic competition, oligopolies, monopsony, and monopoly.

Basically, these markets are segregated on the degree of competition, market share, and control over the market price. This can be depicted through the diagram given below. Monopoly has the greatest degree of control over price and the least number of firms. On the other extreme, perfect competition has the maximum number of firms and zero control of price. All other types of firms lie in the middle.

Perfect Competition

Imagine going to a *sabzi mandi* (local vegetable market). There would be many vegetable vendors trying to sell the same type of vegetables and many people trying to buy vegetables. This is the closest example of a real-life perfectly competitive market. As the name indicates, this market is characterized by a very high degree of competition. The sellers don't actually get to set

MONOPOLY

OLIGOPOLY

MONOPOLISTIC COMPETITION

PERFECT COMPETITION

the prices: instead, they have to agree to a market price that the buyers are willing to pay.

Perfect competition is a market structure that is subject to a very high number of buyers and sellers. All producers sell the exact same products-homogeneous products. Due to the high degree of competition, all firms are said to be price takers, meaning that they cannot set their own prices. This is very intuitive: if any firm increases its price, the quantity demanded of their product will decrease. Hence, they would be driven out of the market. Since the market share of each firm is so small, they have to adhere to the price mechanism to cover all costs of production in the long run. The competition is very high because there are virtually no barriers to entry and exit in the market. High barriers to entry are typically very high initial capital, high fixed costs or unequal market share. When entering and exiting a market is free of cost, more and more people try to enter the market. It is also assumed that everyone in the market has perfect information. Everyone knows what prices are being charged by every firm and every firm knows how much quantity of the product is being demanded in the market.

The absence of government intervention is another characteristic of perfect competition. There are no maximum or minimum price controls, no bans and no taxes on the products. The government also does not pose any barriers to entry or exit in this market form. For instance, there can be free entry and exit of firms in the research and IT-related industries, and governments do not stop people from studying or engaging in research projects.

It is important to note that the concept of perfectly competitive markets is a very theoretical one. Such a market form does not exist in real-life scenarios. Firstly, all market agents never have complete information leading to some degree of unawareness at all times. Secondly, products are not perfectly homogeneous. There are multiple factors such as popularity, efficiency, and intelligence of people employed, and the success of advertising campaigns that lead to some product differentiation. Thirdly, there is always some amount of government intervention in all markets. There may be very low corporation taxes or liberal employment laws, but they do exist.

One of the greatest things about perfectly competitive markets is that the consumers are sovereign. It is their demand for the good that determines the price that is charged in the economy. As we saw earlier, this is known as price mechanism, or more famously Adam Smith's "invisible hand." For this reason, consumers cannot be exploited. If a firm tries to charge higher prices, it will be driven out of the market. If a firm tries to sell poor quality products, it will be driven out of the market due to lower demand. Each firm will have to be allocatively as well as productively efficient. This means that they will have to produce the equilibrium quantity and sell at the equilibrium price. They will also have to produce at the lowest possible cost of production in order to break even. In this manner, perfect competition promotes efficiency in the production process.

Monopoly

Monopoly is another extreme scenario but it is possible in real life. "Mono" means single and "poly" means the seller. So, monopoly means that only one producer has a complete market share. There are extremely high barriers to entry and exit, and the producers can potentially exploit consumers. Think intuitively. If there is only one person who produces a commodity in the whole industry, then you will have to accept whatever price they are charging in order to utilize that product. Since barriers to entry are very high, the market is not subject to any competition. Due to economies of scale, a monopoly can produce and sell at very low costs of production. However, a new firm cannot sell at such a low price without incurring losses. It takes time for a firm to undergo natural growth and eventually benefit from economies of scale in the long run, and this is not possible when the whole market share lies in the hands of just one firm.

Monopoly power can also be granted by the government. In some industries, it is not feasible to have multiple firms competing, so the government gives all the power to just one firm and prevents other firms from entering the market through the use of regulations. For instance, there is no need to have multiple firms in the railways industry since one railway establishment is enough. Similarly, state-owned enterprises may have a monopoly in sectors such as defense where private firms can easily create monopolies and exploit the consumers. The defense industry is not only dangerous but it is also strategic. It is essential that every country have a robust defense mechanism that can be monitored so that national security is maintained.

There are multiple pros and cons of having a private sector monopoly. Firstly, high profits for a firm might enable it to reinvest in research and innovation, which would, in the long run, lead to better quality products being sold in the long run. Production processes may also become more efficient, causing the unit price of the product to decrease. Due to the humongous size of the organization, it is possible for the firm to have plants or franchises in multiple countries, hence adding to the balance of payments credit of the home country. On the contrary, a monopoly can abuse its power by charging abnormally high prices to its consumers and being inefficient, because it knows that it would not be challenged by other potentially efficient firms that cannot enter the market because of higher barriers to entry and exit. For this reason, the government has to make decisions whether it wants to allow monopolies in its economy or whether it wants to prohibit them.

Monopolistic Competition

In Monopolistic Competition, firms offer products or services that are similar, but not perfect substitutes. Since goods can easily be substituted for each other, the price elasticity of demand for the goods sold in monopolistic competition is very high. This is why firms have to adhere to the market price.

Even a small fluctuation from the equilibrium price can cause a considerable loss in revenue of the firm. This means that there is a minute degree of product differentiation. Barriers to entry and exit in a monopolistic competitive industry are low, and the decisions of anyone firm do not directly affect those of its competitors. All firms have a very small market share and they are price takers. One of the most important aspects of monopolistic competition is brand loyalty. Therefore, it can be inferred that it is a market form between perfect competition and a monopoly, which are the two extremes.

Unlike perfect competition, some forms are able to earn profits above normal profit but only in the short run. If a firm earns high profits, companies outside the industry are attracted because of the good prospects. This leads to an increase in competition and the number of suppliers of the commodity causing the profits to decrease. Such short-run increases in profits can be earned through advertisement campaigns and through spreading information about the product. Monopolistic competition is a form of competition that characterizes a number of industries that are familiar to consumers in their day-to-day lives. Examples include restaurants, hair salons, clothing, and consumer electronics.

Firms in monopolistic competition expend large amounts real resources on advertising and other forms of marketing. When there is a real difference between the products of different firms, which the consumer might not be aware of, these expenditures can be useful. However, if it is instead the case that the products are near-perfect substitutes, which is likely in monopolistic competition, then real resources spent on advertising and marketing end up being wasteful.

Oligopoly

An oligopoly is a market structure where a small number of firms have a substantial chunk of the market share. The concentration ratio is a measure of the number of firms in a market. A monopoly would have just one firm: a duopoly will have two firms and so on. The most important characteristic of this market structure is that each firm's actions in an oligopoly affect the decisions made by another firm. This is because there is such a small number of firms that "mainly" sell the product. Many daily appliances and groceries are sold by oligopolies. For instance, take the toothpaste industry. There are very few sellers such as Pepsodent, Colgate, and Meswak that "mainly" sell toothpaste. From this, it implies that Pepsodent's pricing, advertising, and retail strategies are dependent on Colgate's pricing and marketing strategies. This is studied through game theory.

An industry has an oligopoly when the barriers to entry and exit are very high. The initial capital required to set up a firm, the cost of land, and machinery, or the cost of required skills is extremely high. It can be noted, however, that advent of modern technology has changed these requirements to some extent. Traditional office spaces are not required, learning has been made easy from numerous online courses and degrees and much more.

Such a set up of 3 or more firms having a major market share is stable primarily because all firms see the benefit of collaborating over being in actual market competition. This can be done in 2 ways. The first way is price-fixing where firms set the price of a product or service, rather than allowing it to be determined naturally through free-market forces. Price-fixing (also known as colluding) is illegal; however, it is also very difficult to detect because goods and services sold in oligopolies are fairly similar. The second way is through price leadership. This occurs when one powerful firm in an industry is able to influence the overall price of a market and is generally practiced in a market with large-sized firms. In a dominant price leadership, one firm has a large part of market share and so, whatever prices they set have to be followed by other smaller firms if they want to remain in business. They might also engage in predatory pricing in order to drive other firms out of competition. Since they are producing at such a large scale they can afford to have a very low unit price in contrast to the smaller firms in the industry. A firm can also become a price leader if it is better at anticipating the consumer demands and preferences, in which case it would be most beneficial for the other firms to follow its footsteps.

When firms in an oligopoly are collaborating, each firm has an incentive to cheat. Let's take an example. Imagine that in the chips industry, Lays, Cornitos, and Uncle Chips decide to restrict the supply of chips to drive the price of chips higher. Although all of them would benefit from higher prices, cheating would enable one of the companies to earn a substantial market share. Game theorists model this through the prisoner's dilemma. When costs and benefits are balanced so that no firm wants to break from the group, it is considered the "Nash equilibrium" state, wherein a change in the behavior of one of the firms would create a loss for the other.

Larry and David got arrested for dealing drugs, and are being interrogated in separate rooms and cannot communicate.

The Drug Enforcement Agency does not have any other witnesses and can only solve the case by making one of the two suspects tell the truth and betray their accomplice. They have been given a choice between remaining silent and/or to rat the person out. If they decide to rat the person out and testify in court, they will get a smaller sentence of one year. If one testifies and the other does not, then the one who testifies will go free and the other will get three years. If both of them testify, then both of them will get a two-year sentence. From Larry's point of view, if David does not rat him out then both of them could do one year in jail. However, David will be better off by defecting and going free. The same dilemma is faced by David too. If both of them remain loyal to each other, they will be in a "Nash equilibrium," but defecting will always make them better off.

Such a dilemma generally leads to "tragedy of the commons" when everyone neglects the repercussions of their actions on the society in the pursuit of personal gain. This leads to negative externalities and scarce resources get depleted and this is a loss for everyone.

	DAVID confess	DAVID deny
LARRY confess	Larry – 2 years David – 2 years	Larry – 3 years David – FREE !!!
LARRY deny	Larry – FREE !! David – 3 years	Larry – free with a fine David – free with a fine.

#1   #2   #3

Chapter- 4
UTILITY THEORY
& INDIFFERENCE CURVES

Chapter 4

UTILITY THEORY AND INDIFFERENCE CURVES

Let's go back to Nero's Truly Lemon Lemonade. Say you went for a long run and now you are parched. You come across his little store and go a little overboard and purchase 4 lemonades. The first lemonade will give you maximum satisfaction but as you drink the second one, the satisfaction that you will derive from it would be lesser than that of the first one. Similarly, the satisfaction would be even lesser when you would drink the third one and your stomach will probably start hurting if you drink the last lemonade. It can be noticed that the satisfaction derived decreases as the quantity of the lemonade consumed increases.

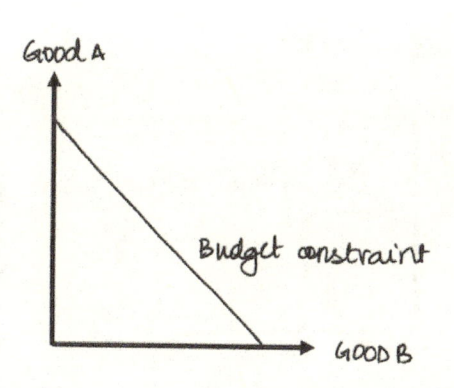

Utility can be defined as the satisfaction derived from consuming a good or a service. It is difficult to measure since it is a very subjective variable; however, economists measure utility in terms of "utils," which is its unit. The previous example was an actualization of the law of diminishing marginal utility. The law states that as the quantity consumed increases, the total utility increases but at a diminishing rate. In simpler words, utility from using each successive unit of product has less utility as compared to the last one. The fancy term used for "additional utility from each successive unit of product" is marginal utility.

Remember how we studied about the production possibility curve in which the maximum quantity of 2 goods that can be produced with given resources is plotted on the x-y plane. Similarly, an indifference curve plots the combinations of 2 commodities that leave a consumer with the same amount of satisfaction. This implies that every point on an indifference curve has the same total utility. It must also be noted that on each indifference curve, the consumer has an equal preference for the 2 goods. For instance, a little boy might have the same preference for comic books and toy cars.

Typically, 2 indifference curves would never intersect. This is because different indifference curves show different levels of total satisfaction. So, if 2 indifference curves ever were to intersect, it would mean that the same bundle of goods provides 2 levels of satisfaction! This obviously doesn't make any sense. Moreover, higher indifference curves or indifference curves that are far from the origin depict a higher level of total satisfaction.

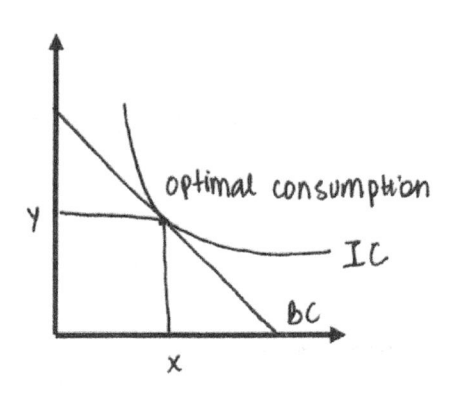

A budget constraint shows the income level of a consumer. It is a line that contains the combinations of 2 goods that could be purchased with a given income. A budget constraint for a higher income level would be further from the origin. Optimal consumption occurs at the point where the budget constraint is a tangent to an indifference curve. The optimal consumption point shows the quantity of 2 goods that could be bought with the given income and would give the maximum satisfaction at that income level.

Marginal Rate of Substitution

The indifference curve also shows the marginal rate of substitution. It is generally downward-sloping and convex to the origin. The marginal rate of substitution is the amount of a good that a consumer is willing to consume in relation to another good. The assumption here is that the goods are perfect substitutes and that the consumer is indifferent between them.

To know the marginal rate of substitution at a given quantity of both the goods, a tangent is drawn at the desired point and the slope is calculated. The slope itself is the marginal rate of substitution. Since the indifference curve is literally a "curve," the tangent is changing at every point on the curve; it follows that the marginal rate of substitution is also changing continuously.

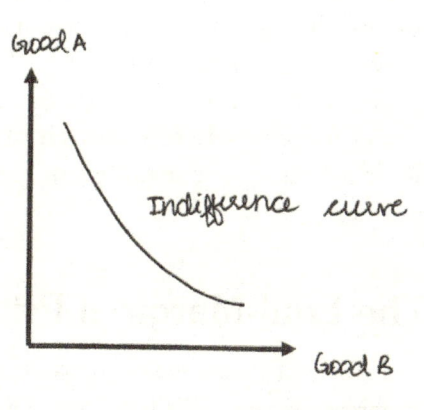

The shape of the indifference curve also talks a lot about the trend in MRS along the indifference curve because as you consume more of one good you will consume less of the other. This explains the convex shape of the indifference curve. If an indifference curve were to be a straight line, then the marginal rate of substitution would be constant as the slope of a straight line is constant. Indifference curves that are concave to the origin are rather uncommon. A concave indifference curve shows that as a consumer increases the consumption of cone goods, he also simultaneously increases the consumption of another good. This is an uncommon phenomenon. Conversely, in real-life settings, marginal substitution is diminishing. In order to increase consumption of one good, the consumption of another good would decrease as the consumer will substitute one good for another.

The law of diminishing marginal rates of substitution states that MRS decreases as one moves down a standard convex-shaped curve, which is the indifference curve. Hence, the marginal rate of substitution forms a downward, negative sloping, convex curve that shows one good being replaced for another good. The MRS curve only compares 2 goods. However, in practice, a larger basket of goods is purchased by consumers. Moreover, the theory assumes that the consumer is indifferent between the chosen goods. This might not be true and the consumer might prefer one product over another.

The Equi-Marginal Principle

The study of utility theory is particularly important in order to understand consumer behavior. The fact that we want to make the maximum benefit out of any given situation is basic human nature. It follows that given 2 types of goods, consumers will choose a combination of goods that maximizes their total utility. This is the equi-marginal principle.

It can be mathematically represented as:

Marginal utility of A/Price of A = Marginal utility of B/Price of B = Marginal utility of B/Price of B

This is pretty intuitive because the value of MU/P decreases as the price of A (PA) increases. This means that the marginal utility per dollar spent decreases if the price of the item were to increase. Since the aim is to make the maximum benefit, the consumer spends less of good A and more on other goods.

There are a number of assumptions that are made for this principle to be true. The consumers are considered to be rational and would always seek to maximize profits. They would also have a fixed amount of income. Here, utility is described in cardinal terms (in the form of money). Henceforth, the consumer would naturally consider their marginal utility of the product as well as the price of the product while making a purchase. Unconsciously, they would be applying the equi-marginal principle in order to decide whether or not they would purchase the good or not.

Although the principle might seem obvious and perfectly "in place" for real-life scenarios, it has many limitations. Firstly, the concept of utility is very subjective and it is hard to assign monetary values to the amount of satisfaction one will get from consuming a good. Moreover, consumers don't actually apply the equi-marginal principle consciously while making a purchase. Instead, they just buy a good out of habit or out of gut feeling. The fact that consumers are always rational is a very big and a very absurd assumption to make. The choices that consumers make might be influenced by factors such as brand loyalty, information failure, and advertisements. The marginal utility theory itself is limited by the fact that only 2 goods can't be analyzed at a time. In real life, there are numerous goods that are bought and sold, and their prices are also very dynamic in nature.

Income and Substitution Effect

So you work in Walmart and Christmas is close, so your manager gives you a pay raise. Now that you have more money in your pocket, your purchasing power has increased. Since you have more money, you would obviously buy yourself more presents. Your purchasing power has increased. Conversely, if you experience a salary cut, you will have less money and would purchase a smaller quantity of goods.

This effect of changes in consumption because of changes in income is known as the income effect. Income effect can be direct or indirect. When a consumer chooses to make changes to the way he or she spends because of a change in income, the income effect is said to be direct. However, when there are changes in patterns of spending because of changes in other factors, the change is said to be indirect. Imagine that the market price of avocados has risen. Earlier you would've bought 5 avocados while grocery shopping, but now you can only purchase 3 because your purchasing power has fallen. The income effect can be explained using the concept of Marginal Propensity to Consume. It is a concept based on the balance between the spending and saving habits of consumers. The marginal propensity to consume is included in a larger theory of macroeconomics known as Keynesian economics.

In the previous chapter, we have already seen what substitute goods are (two goods that can easily replace each other). When you experience a pay raise, you substitute low price products for more expensive and better quality products. For instance, following a pay raise, you decide to replace your Android mobile phone for a new iPhone 12. This leads to a decrease in the consumption of Android phones and an increase in the consumption of iPhones. The inverse is true when incomes decrease. When you are low on budget, you would prefer to purchase cheaper goods instead of more expensive goods. Here, it is important to note that we are assuming that the good is a normal good and its demand increases when the price of the good decreases.

While the substitution effect changes consumption patterns in favor of the more affordable alternative, even a modest reduction in price may make a more expensive product more attractive to consumers. If airplane ticket prices are high and train prices are low, consumers would naturally prefer to travel using a train if budget is a concern. However, if the airplane ticket prices fell a little bit, people would be more attracted to travel using an airplane.

Interestingly, the substitution effect is not limited to consumption. It also comes into play when firms outsource parts of their operations. Using cheap labor in poorer countries can have a benefit for the companies because they are substituting cheap labor for expensive labor at home. However, the benefit for those laborers would be negative because they would be earning far less than what laborers in other developed economies would.

In order to graphically analyze income and substitution effect, we draw budget constraints and indifference curves on the same axis. Income effect causes the budget constraint to shift, causing the "optimum consumption" point to shift too. Hence, income effect can be graphically depicted as a shift to a new indifference curve. On the other hand, the substitution effect is the change that would occur if the consumer were required to remain on the original indifference curve and hence can be shown as a movement along an indifference curve.

Costs and Revenue

Suppose you have a business. What would your main aim be? Obviously, it would be to create the maximum amount of money possible. You would not want any losses and would prefer to have a greater return than investment. With the production process comes some costs and benefits to the firm. The benefits are in the form of revenue for the firm. In order to find the profit (i.e., the net revenue), the revenue is subtracted from the cost.

Costs

A firm's explicit costs comprise all explicit payments to the factors of production that the firm uses. For instance, if you buy land, you pay rent. If you employ people, you give them wages and salaries. If you invest in a machine, you pay interest. On the other hand, a firm's implicit cost consists of the opportunity cost of using the firm's own resources, without receiving any explicit compensation for those resources. For example, the opportunity cost of having a coffee business would be to have a business in tea.

Costs can also be categorized in the form of fixed and variable costs. In the short run, some of the input factors that the firm uses are fixed. It would be extremely difficult to shift a factory plant to a new location in a short period of time. In the same manner, some workers might be on a six-month or one year contract with the firm, so in the short run, those employees would be categorized as permanent labor.

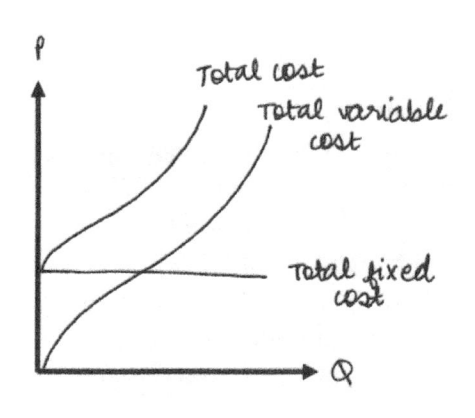

The entrepreneur will have to bear the fixed costs even if the output is zero.

Think about it. You will still have to pay the rent for your factory even if you are not doing anything on the land.

Variable cost is the cost that depends on the quantity of output produced. The cost of raw materials is a variable cost because it would be zero if the firm is not producing any output. In the long run, all costs are variable costs because all the factors of production can be changed in the long run.

A firm's total cost of production is the sum of all its variable and fixed costs. It is basically the amount of money you will need to have the business functioning in the first place. The firm's marginal cost is the per unit change in total cost that results from a change in quantity produced. In simpler words, it is the additional cost of producing one more unit of output.

Revenue

Revenue is the money that a firm gains through the sale of its products. Average revenue is the revenue generated from selling one unit of output. Average revenue is the same as the price. Similarly, marginal revenue (also known as a marginal product) is the addition to total revenue from selling one more unit of output.

The profit earned by a firm is the positive difference between the costs and the revenue of the firm.

1. **Accounting profit**: accounting profits are the firm's total revenues from sales of its output minus the firm's explicit costs. The firm's opportunity cost of producing a product is not taken into account.

2. **Economic profits**: economic profits are the total revenue minus explicit and implicit costs. This is the same as the difference between accounting profits and the implicit cost of production.

"Normal profit" is a term used to describe a situation where the economic profit is zero. This means that the firm is covering all of its costs but it does not have any retained profits. The implicit costs keep adding up to the profits of the firm that it would "normally" receive if it were properly compensated for the use of resources. "Supernormal Profits" or abnormal profits can be described as "profit of a firm over and above what provides its owners with a normal return to capital." This means they are not merely breaking even but are actually earning extra money.

Relationship Between Marginal Cost and Marginal Product

The marginal cost falls at first, then starts to rise. This behavior is a consequence of the relationship between marginal cost and marginal product and the law of diminishing returns. As we studied before, the law of diminishing returns states that there is a decrease in the marginal output of a production process as the amount of a single factor of production incrementally increases, *ceteris paribus*.

As the marginal product of the variable input–labor rises, the firm's total product increases at a rate that is greater than the rate of new workers hired. Consequently, the firm's marginal costs will be decreasing. Eventually, the law of diminishing returns kicks in and the marginal product of the variable factor will begin to decline. This gives the average cost curve and the total cost curve a U-shape.

Chapter - 5
GOVERNMENT'S MICROECONOMIC INTERVENTION

Chapter 5

GOVERNMENT'S MICROECONOMIC INTERVENTION

The main purpose of governments intervening in market processes is to address market failures and inefficiencies. Let's first look at different kinds of efficiencies and what the ideal situation would look like.

No set threshold determines the effectiveness of an economy, but indicators of economic efficiency include goods brought to market at the lowest possible cost and labor that provides the greatest possible output.

Development in technology often complements increases in economic efficiency. For example, steam engines and motor vehicles that emerged during the Industrial Revolution reduced travel time and increased efficiency in trade. New sources of energy such as fossil fuels were also introduced and were cheaper, more effective, and more versatile.

Movements such as the Industrial Revolution also brought efficiencies in time. Discovery of industrial machinery and the "factory system" not only increased the output but also reduced the time taken to produce a given quantity of goods. We say that the productivity of the production process has increased as the "output per worker hour" increases. A famous example in popular culture of the quest for efficiency is the biographical novel "Cheaper by the Dozen" by Frank Bunker Gilbreth, Jr. and Ernestine Gilbreth Carey. In the book, Gilbreth Jr. develops systems to maximize efficiency in even the most mundane tasks, such as brushing your teeth.

Efficiency

In microeconomics, economic efficiency is a situation in which nothing can be improved without something else being hurt. There are two main areas of thought when it comes to economic efficiency. One focuses on the distortions created by governments and believe that reduced government intervention would increase efficiency. The second focuses on the distortions created by market forces and believe that increased government intervention would lead to increased efficiency.

Efficiency leads to a larger quantity of goods being produced at a lower unit price. Advances as a result of efficiency have facilitated higher standards of living such as supplying homes with electricity, running water, and giving people the ability to travel. Efficiency is an important attribute because all inputs are scarce. Time, money, and raw materials are limited, and it is important to conserve them while maintaining an acceptable level of output.

Efficiency can be of three types: allocative or Pareto efficiency, dynamic efficiency, and productive efficiency. We will be looking at these in the next section.

Allocative Efficiency

Allocative efficiency is the property of an efficient market whereby all goods and services are optimally distributed among buyers in an economy. It occurs when consumers pay a market price that reflects the private marginal cost of production. The condition for allocative efficiency for a firm is to produce an output where marginal cost, MC, just equals price, P. In other words, when every good or service is produced up to the point where one more unit provides a marginal benefit to consumers less than the marginal cost of producing it.

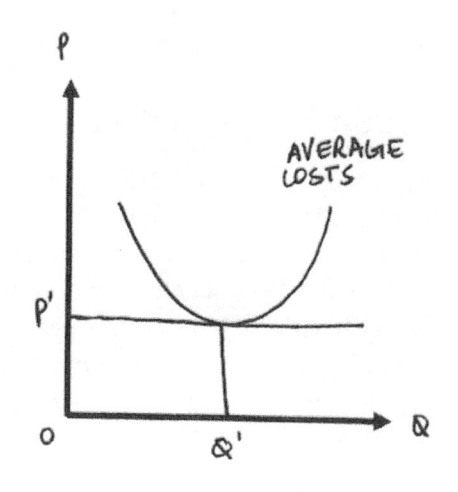

As we studied in the previous chapters, the quantity at which the demand equals supply is known as the equilibrium quantity and the price is known as equilibrium price. When the market price is the same as the equilibrium price, there is no surplus or shortage and the market clears. Since there's no wastage of any kind, the market is said to be allocatively efficient.

A very important aspect of allocative efficiency is the availability of information. When all of the data affecting a market is available for use in decisions, companies can make accurate decisions which would be beneficial and rewarding. In order to be allocationally efficient, a market must be efficient overall. An efficient market is one in which all pertinent data regarding the market and its activities is readily available to all market participants and is always reflected in market prices. In order for a market to be efficient, it must meet the prerequisites of being both informationally efficient and transactionally efficient (when a market is transactionally efficient, all transaction costs are reasonable and fair, making all transactions equally executable by all parties).

Productive Efficiency

We already know that resources are scarce and wants are unlimited. When the demand for a given good rises, producers naturally produce more of that good. There comes a point at which the producer cannot produce more of that product without having to reduce the production of another good or without incurring losses. The point where the firm makes zero losses and functions at max capacity is called the productively efficient point.

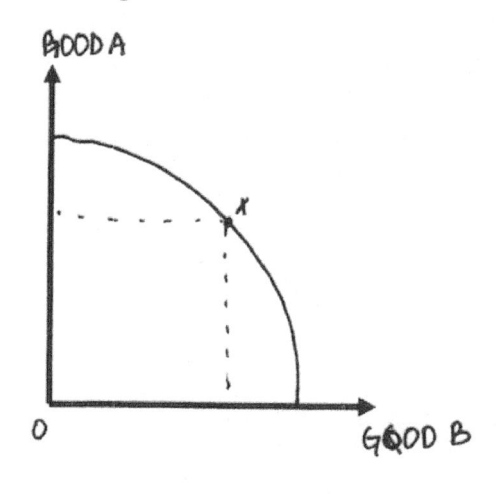

Generally, the concept of production efficiency centers around the charting of a production possibility frontier (PPF). A point beyond the PPF is imaginary and one inside the PPF is productively inefficient because the firm would have spare capacity. At maximum production efficiency, an entity cannot produce any additional units without drastically altering its portfolio of production to gain added capacity capabilities through lowering the production of another product. Productive efficiency is, therefore, the minimum point of an average cost curve.

It is essential to note that productivity serves as a measurement of output, normally expressed as some units per amount of time, such as 100 units per hour. Efficiency in production most often relates to the costs per unit of production rather than just the number of units produced.

Productive efficiency can be increased dramatically through increased government expenditure on healthcare and education. This not only increases the productive potential of laborers but also increases their productivity.

Dynamic Efficiency

Dynamic efficiency is basically productive efficiency in the long run. A firm that is dynamically efficient will be reducing its cost curves by implementing new production processes. Dynamic efficiency is commonly associated with "technological progressiveness and innovation" as this lowers the "average total cost" curve and makes the production process more efficient as a whole. Remember how I said previously, "Efficiency is a situation in which nothing can be improved without something else being hurt." The whole concept of dynamic efficiency is the same but in the long run. For this reason, dynamic efficiency involves a trade-off. The money that would be spent on creating better technology could have potentially been used on better infrastructure or healthcare. Dynamic efficiency may also involve implementing better working practices and better management of human capital. Labor unions are powerful in economies that are dynamically efficient.

Multiple factors influence dynamic efficiency. They are:

- Rapid development of technology can enable firms to produce more for lower costs
- Investment in new technology and improved capital can enable lower costs in future
- Access to finance will enable firms to invest in new capital which will enable lower costs

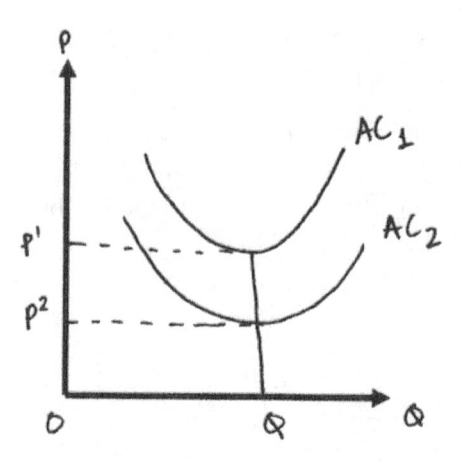

A brilliant example of a firm increasing its dynamic efficiency is Ford. They made an extremely efficient use of production lines and "breaking down the production process." Throughout the 1920s and 30s, Ford was the most efficient car-producer. However, by the 1950s and 60s, it was starting to lose its competitive advantage as Japanese car firms innovated and improved the quality of car-building. Similarly, Yahoo used to be the dominant search engine, but it quickly lost its position to a new entrant–Google.

Let us now look into the various instruments that the government uses to intervene in markets.

Taxation

A tax is a payment made to the government. It is the money from taxes that the governments use to provide public goods and services such as street lights, healthcare, public schools, etc. A tax base refers to the population of a country that is supposed to pay taxes. A larger tax base leads to larger tax revenue. Tax systems have varied considerably across jurisdictions and time. In most modern systems, taxation occurs on both physical assets such as property and specific events such as a sales transaction. These are known as direct and indirect taxes, respectively. We will be looking into each of these types in-depth.

Why Tax?

The most basic function of taxation is to fund government expenditures. Varying justifications and explanations for taxes have been offered throughout history. Earlier, kings used to tax their people to gain money for their own use and for armies. Later, when the concept of democracy was understood by more and more people around the world, governments would tax their people to reduce income inequality and redistribute earnings for spending on public goods and more. Taxes have also been used to discourage spending on demerit goods such as gasoline (which causes pollution), cigarettes (that cause cancer), and alcohol. Subsequently, the money earned from taxing such goods is spent on merit goods such as education, healthcare, and infrastructure development.

Direct Taxation

If you ever paid attention, you must've seen your parents file their income taxes or you might have seen Donald Trump and Joe Biden indulge in a heated discussion about tax rates in the United States. These are all payments made to the government that is a proportion of the total income earned from work. These can be made by an individual or a company to the government. The "Ability to pay Principle" states that those who have more resources or earn a higher income should pay more taxes. Conversely, the "ability to charge principle" is a way to redistribute the wealth of a nation. Direct taxes cannot be passed onto a different person or entity; the individual or organization upon whom or which the tax is levied is responsible for the fulfillment of the full tax payment.

Very high direct tax rates have been a cause of disincentive to work and enterprise. Why wouldn't it be? People spend hours and hours in their offices just to pay 30% of what they've earned to be just given away? When taxes are very high, the rate of tax evasion is also high. People end up lying in their tax statements or delaying their payments as far as possible. For this reason, a perfect balance is crucial. Income tax, corporate tax (also known as capital gains tax), inheritance tax, and property tax are some examples of direct taxes and are levied directly on a person or a business. Let's look at each of them in detail.

1. **Income Tax**

    It is based on one's income. A certain percentage is taken from a worker's salary, depending on how much he or she earns. A personal income tax is levied on wages, salaries, and other types of income. A business income tax is levied on corporations, partnerships, small businesses, and people who are self-employed. The money generated from income taxes is generally reinvested in a country through various public schemes.

2. **Capital Gains Tax**

    Capital gains tax, as the name suggests, is levied when a person "gains" from the sale of a non-inventory asset. These can include stocks, bonds, gold, real estate, and property. The tax rate of the capital gains tax depends on how much profit you gained and also on what your income is.

3. **Inheritance Tax**

    An inheritance tax is a tax paid by a person who inherits money or property of a person who has died. This is the tax that the PERSON has to pay and must not be confused with estate tax, which is levied ON the property and money that is being inherited.

4. **Property Tax**

   Property tax is charged on properties such as land and buildings and is used for maintaining public services such as the police and fire departments, schools and libraries, as well as roads.

Indirect Taxes

Indirect taxes are not directly paid to the government. Instead, they are collected by an agent in the supply chain, generally a firm or retail store, and then are paid to the government. The cool thing about these kinds of taxes is that they can be passed on to the consumer. Whether or not this can happen depends on the price elasticity of demand for the product being sold. If the demand is price inelastic, people would still be willing to purchase the good at a higher price. This means that if the government decides to levy a very high sales tax or GST, the sellers can easily extract the amount in the form of higher prices. On the other hand, if the demand for the product is price elastic, the consumers will significantly cut consumption if the sellers try to charge high prices in order to cover up for the tax. There are multiple kinds of sales taxes:

1. **Sales Tax**

    Sales tax is added to whatever you are buying. The sales price is the cost price of the product plus tax. This is levied on everyday items such as groceries, toiletries, books, etc.

2. **Excise Tax**

    When a manufacturer buys the raw materials for the company's products, for example, tobacco for cigarette companies, they already need to pay indirect taxes on the items. However, it can be noted that since the demand for cigarettes is inelastic (it's addictive), the manufacturers can transfer the tax burden onto the consumers.

3. **Customs Tax**

    This is also sometimes referred to as tariff. Whenever you purchase something from an international brand and import it to your home country, you pay an additional fee known as customs tax.

    Indirect taxes are particularly efficient because they are hard to evade, since they are charged when goods are purchased. Indirect taxes on goods that are price inelastic can boost a government's tax revenue. Moreover, indirect taxes such as sales tax and excise tax can significantly discourage the consumption of demerit goods.

4. **Value-Added Tax (VAT)**

    Throughout the production process, value is added to the product at every stage. For example, value is added to a ball of cotton when it is weaved and turned into a cotton cloth. Similarly, more value is added when the cloth becomes a t-shirt and has a brand. A value-added tax is a consumption tax placed on a product whenever the value is added at each stage of the supply chain, from production to the point of sale.

Tax Rates and Different Taxation Systems

The tax system can be progressive, regressive or proportional. In a progressive tax system, the tax rate increases as an individual's wealth increases. This reduces income inequality as the people with higher incomes pay higher taxes and those with lower incomes pay lower taxes. A good example of a progressive tax system is the US Federal Tax System. Here, each dollar the individual earns places him into a bracket or category, resulting in a higher tax rate once the dollar amount hits a new threshold. Conversely, in a regressive tax system, the rate of tax increases as the income decreases. Low-income individuals pay a higher amount of their incomes in taxes compared to high-income earners under a regressive tax system. You might now be wondering why would a government put a regressive tax? Well, sales taxes such as the GST are regressive in nature. A $2 tax on a $15 t-shirt would be a higher proportion of income for a factory worker and almost nothing for a millionaire. So, the marginal rate of tax on the person with a lower income is greater than that of a richer person. The third type of tax system is the proportional tax system. It is also known as a flat tax and the rate of tax is the same for all income groups. It's meant to create equality between marginal tax rates and average tax rates paid. Proponents of proportional taxes believe they stimulate the economy by encouraging people to work more because there is no tax penalty for earning more.

Government's Price Controls

If you ever did any part-time job at a Subway or a cafeteria, you would've been paid the minimum wage. This minimum wage is a price control put by the government in the labor market. Price controls are usually implemented as a means of direct economic intervention to manage the affordability of certain goods. When prices are established by the market forces in a free market, they shift to maintain the balance between supply and demand.

However, when a maximum or a minimum price control is levied, the equilibrium is not reached and there is a surplus or a deficit. This means that price controls would inevitably lead to market failure.

Let us now look at the various kinds of price controls that a government can levy in an economy.

1. **Minimum price**

    A minimum price is when the government doesn't allow prices to go below a certain level. If minimum prices are set above the equilibrium, it will cause an increase in prices. If the quantity demanded would be less than the quantity supplied, there would be a surplus in the market. A minimum price is also referred to as a price floor, meaning that the price cannot fall below the "floor" that is set by the government. For example, a government might pose a minimum price on the agricultural goods produced in the economy to support their farmers.

2. **Maximum Price**

    Maximum price, also known as the price ceiling, is levied by the government when it wishes to prevent prices from going above a certain level. However, if the price is below the equilibrium level, the quantity demanded will be greater than the quantity supplied. This would cause a shortage in the economy.

The government might want to use maximum price controls when it wishes to reduce the cost of a given good. This is often done in the housing market in order to make the cost of renting a house lower. The problem with doing this is that people have to wait in order to get a house as the demand for a house is way larger than the number of houses available.

3. **Direct Price Setting**

You might be wondering how prices are set in countries such as Russia and China, which are command or communist economies. Since all the decision-making power is in the hands of the government to decide how to produce, what to produce, and the prices that are to be charged in the market. This phenomena is known as direct price setting.

4. **Price Bands**

In some economies, the government does not necessarily fix a rigid maximum or minimum price. Instead, it allows the price to fluctuate between given boundaries. In order to prevent the price from exceeding these boundaries, the government keeps "buffer stocks." A buffer stock is the price control where the government seeks to keep the price within a certain band. It effectively combines the elements of maximum and minimum prices without completely removing the market forces from the scenario.

This can be achieved in the agriculture industry. For example, the government of country X purchases a certain quantity of the agricultural produce. It then purchases or sells more of this product and keeps its price between the given band in case the prices change dramatically.

Subsidies

A subsidy is a benefit given to an individual, business, or institution, usually by the government. Subsidies can be given in the form of direct payments or in the form of tax reductions. The main purpose of giving subsidies is to reduce some burden or to help out a business. For instance, a government may subsidize gas cylinders so that the economically disadvantaged people in the country don't have to use firewood to cook food.

Direct subsidies involve an actual payment of funds to a particular individual or a company.

Indirect subsidies, on the other hand, don't have a predefined monetary value. They are transmitted into the market in the form of lower prices and sales tax reductions.

Let us now dive in to look at the different kinds of subsidies that are provided by the government in developed economies.

1. **Welfare Payments**

    Welfare payments include a range of government programs that provide financial aid to individuals who cannot support themselves. Social welfare systems provide assistance to individuals and families through programs such as healthcare, food stamps, unemployment compensation, housing assistance, and childcare assistance. The main purpose behind these payments is to promote work, education, and for developed economies, a better standard of life.

    It is important to note that such welfare payments are financed through taxation. When there is a higher rate of tax evasion and a very low rate of tax on the incomes of people, the government has a very low tax revenue. Obviously, they would then have a little money to spend on the welfare of people.

2. Unemployment Benefits

Unemployment benefit is the most common type of government welfare program. It is an insurance benefit that is paid as a result of a person's inability to be employed.

Generally, an unemployment benefit is only provided to somebody who is currently looking for a new job. Moreover, the beneficiary must have worked for at least one quarter in the previous financial year to claim these benefits.

In the United States, Massachusetts provides one of the highest maximum weekly benefits of $742 per week and an additional $25 per child. Conversely, the lowest weekly benefit is provided in Florida at only $275 per week.

What is Massachusetts doing wrong?

Very high unemployment benefits can be fatal for an economy. This is because they would act as a disincentive to work and enterprise. Obviously, why would you want to work if you could just eat off of the government's money?

3. Affordable Care Act

The Affordable Care Act was a healthcare reform signed into law by President Barack Obama in 2010. It expanded Medicaid eligibility and created a health insurance marketplace. It also prevented health insurance companies from denying coverage due to pre-existing conditions and covers a list of essential health benefits.

4. Student Loans

This one might be the most relevant welfare payment for you. Education loan is the sum of money borrowed to finance higher education-related expenses.

Education loans are intended to cover the cost of tuition, books, supplies, and living expenses while the borrower is in the process of pursuing a degree. There are two basic types of education loans: federal loans sponsored by the government and private loans. These loans are generally repaid after the beneficiary has gained education and is in the workforce. A number of employers integrate student loan payment benefits into their employee benefit programs in order to increase the support available for managing the student loan debt after college.

Chapter - 6
MACROECONOMICS

Chapter 6

MACROECONOMICS

Until now, we have looked at individual firms in different situations and the factors affecting their behavior. From now on we will be looking at the economy as a whole. "Macro" means large, and what economics means you know by now. In this branch of economics, performance, structure, behavior, and decision-making of an economy as a whole is studied. In this segment, we will be looking at GDP, unemployment rates, national income, international trade, and international finance. Before we actually get into the study of macroeconomics, we must understand what the "circular flow of income means". Every day we make some sort of economic transactions.

Let's look at this scenario. You purchase a PS4. This means that you are the consumer and you're consuming the PS4. When you purchase it you are paying money to the company. The business then uses that money to pay for the various factors of production such as wages for the laborers, rent for the shop and so on. It is these laborers who would then have money and would be able to consume other goods and services. Money flows in a circular cycle in the economy and keeps changing hands constantly. In an economy, one man's expenditure is another man's income. Sometimes, money leaves the circular flow. When this happens it is known as a withdrawal. Some examples of such outflows include taxes that are paid to the government and savings (money that is stored for later use). Conversely, money can also enter the circular flow of income and this is known as an injection into the economy. These could be subsidies by the government, purchase of domestic goods on the international market and more.

Since we are dealing with the economy as a whole, we talk of "aggregate demand" and "aggregate supply." The literal meaning of the work "aggregate" is a whole formed by combining several separate elements. This means that the demand of all individuals in an economy would be aggregate demand and the supply of all individual firms in an economy is the aggregate supply.

Aggregate Demand

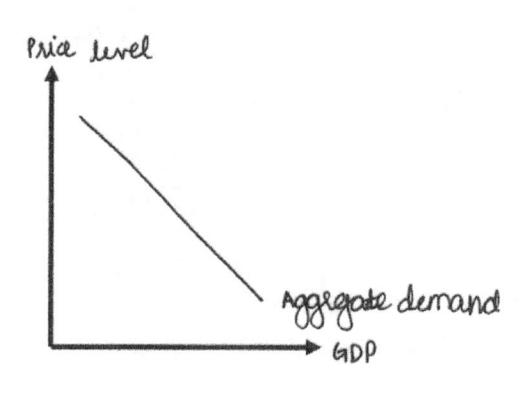

Aggregate demand comprises of the sum of consumption, government expenditure, investment, and net exports. Aggregate demand is the sum of the total spending in an economy over a given time frame. As we have already studied before, demand refers to willingness AND the ability to purchase a product. Here too, it is important to not confuse all the "want" in an economy with all the demand in an economy. The relationship between aggregate demand and the price level might seem similar to the relationship shown in the demand curve for an individual product. There is, however, a significant difference. A demand curve for a product shows the relationship between a change in the relative price of a product and the quantity demanded. The price of the product is changing but it is assumed that the prices of other products have not changed. More of the product is purchased when the price falls, in part because people switch away from rival products.

So, why does aggregate demand also follow the law of demand?

1. The wealth effect: A rise in the price level will reduce the amount of goods and services that people's wealth can buy.

2. The international effect: A rise in the price level will reduce demand for net exports as exports will become less price-competitive while imports will become more price-competitive.

3. The interest rate effect: A rise in the price level will increase the demand for money to pay the higher prices. This, in turn, will increase the interest rate. A higher interest rate usually results in a reduction in consumption and investment.

Aggregate Supply

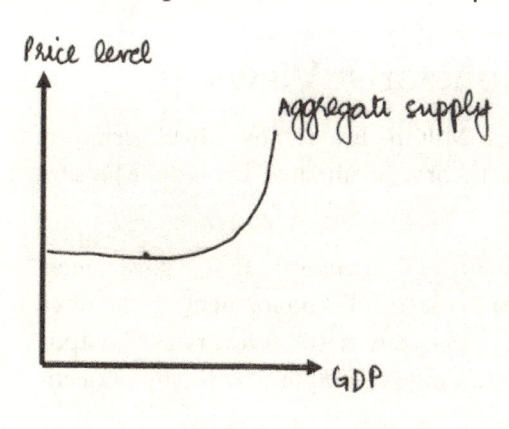

The aggregate supply of a country is the total output (real GDP) that producers in an economy are willing and able to supply at a given price level in a given time period. Short-run aggregate supply (SRAS) is the total output of an economy that will be supplied when there has not been enough time for the prices of factors of production to change. Conversely, the long-run aggregate supply is the total output of a country supplied in the period when prices of factors of production have fully adjusted.

Factors Influencing Aggregate Supply

1. **A change in the price of factors of production:** A rise in wage rates not matched by an increase in labor productivity and raw material costs will cause a decrease in SRAS, shifting the curve to the left as illustrated in Figure 4.4.
2. **A change in taxes on firms**: A reduction in corporation tax or indirect taxes will cause an increase in SRAS.
3. **A change in factor productivity/quality of resources**: A rise in labor productivity and/or capital productivity will cause an increase in aggregate supply both in the short and long run.
4. **A change in the quantity of resources:** In the short run, the supply of inputs may be influenced by supply side shocks including natural disasters. These shocks may not have a significant impact on the productive potential in the long run. The factors that will cause an increase in the quantity of resources, in the long run, will also increase SRAS.

Keynesian vs Monetarist Views

Monetarist economics is Milton Friedman's direct criticism of Keynesian economics theory, formulated by John Maynard Keynes.

The Keynesian theorists maintain that government intervention is needed to achieve full employment. They often represent the LRAS curve as perfectly elastic at low rates of output, then upward sloping over a range of output and finally perfectly inelastic. This causes their long-run supply curve to be a backward-facing L-shape. Neo-classical, or monetarist, economists think that everything should be left to the market forces. According to them, the SRAS curve is a vertical line.

Inflation

Inflation is a general rise in the prices in an economy. One of the government's main aims is to keep the rate of inflation low and constant. This target is generally 2%. This aim, however, coincides with another aim of the government. Economic growth. Growth generally leads to a rise in prices because when people demand more, the suppliers raise their prices.

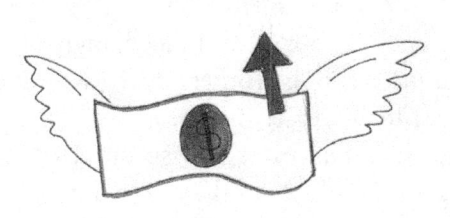

Inflation causes a reduction in the real value of money. For instance, hyperinflation in Venezuela had led to their currency becoming virtually worthless. They had to then adopt the American dollar because people had lost confidence in their own money. If there is inflation and you had previously borrowed money and now have to pay interest on the loan, you might actually be paying less in real terms because the value of money has fallen. This means that borrowers gain and lenders lose as a consequence of inflation. Other costs involved with inflation are the shoe-leather costs and menu costs. Menu costs arise due to changing the price tags and menus when the real prices change. Shoe-leather costs involve the money and time taken up due to moving the money around in different banks to get the best interest rates.

Inflation is of 2 kinds: demand-pull inflation and cost-push inflation

1. **Demand-Pull Inflation**

    If there is an increase in the aggregate demand of a country, more must be supplied so that a new equilibrium is formed. What if the country doesn't have enough resources to produce more? There would be a scarcity of those finished goods. Scarcity would drive up their price and cause demand-pull inflation. Hence, inflation caused by increases in aggregate demand not matched by equivalent increases in aggregate supply is known as demand-pull inflation. This is also sometimes referred to as "good inflation" as it pushes the economy to expand.

2. **Cost-push Inflation**

    This occurs when prices are pushed up by increases in the cost of production. It means that the production process is becoming more and more inefficient due to structural problems. This is bad inflation and is not self-correcting. There are a number of costs that may rise. For instance, wages may increase more than labor productivity and so result in a rise in labor costs. Indeed, higher wages can cause a wage-price spiral. Workers gain a wage rise, which causes prices to increase: then workers seek higher wages to restore their real value and so on. This may also happen because of increases in the prices of raw materials such as oil, gasoline, etc.

High inflation can cause the currency of a country to devalue. This would mean that foreigners would find our exports cheap and would purchase more. This could improve our net exports and could decrease what is known as a "current account deficit."

Going overboard, however, is only fatal for an economy and a balance must be found.

Gross Domestic Product

GDP is a good way to compare the performance of different countries as it measures the total domestic output. The main components of GDP are consumption, investment, government expenditure, and the foreign balance of trade. This means that all four sectors of the economy are included. The following are some terminology that you must know in order to study macroeconomics.

1. **Nominal GDP:** Nominal GDP is evaluated at current market prices in US dollars. It is not adjusted for inflation.

2. **GDP PPP:** PPP here stands for purchasing power parity. For instance, a big Mac would cost more in the United States than it would cost in India. To correct for this difference, a basket of goods are created and weighted. It is intended to adjust for the differences in local prices and cost of living in different countries.

3. **Real GDP:** Real GDP is an inflation-adjusted measure to flex the quantity of goods and services produced by an economy in a given year. Another year with few economic fluctuations is considered to be the base year. Compared to that year, Real GDP is measured.

4. **GDP per capita:** If people capita is found by dividing GDP by the population of a country, it indicates the amount of output per person in an economy.

Economic Growth

Economic growth refers to an increase in the real GDP per capita, often economy, and is reflected by and the overall improvement in the quality of life in a given country. It is important to note that such growth occurs exponentially. This means that the new growth builds up on the past growth through the process of compounding. There are two kinds of economic growth: actual and potential. Actual economic growth occurs when the market value of all goods and services produced in a country increases over time. This causes a movement inside the production possibilities frontier. Potential economic growth occurs when an economy is capable of producing a larger quantity of goods and services than what it is producing right now.

A country can increase its economic growth through employing more physical capital and by accumulating more units of labor. However, this only works until a point. The Cobb Douglas aggregate production function, which relates

GDP to the physical capital accumulation, total units of labor, and the level of technology in a country, is subject to the law of diminishing marginal product. In other words, the marginal contribution of a factor of production to the GDP diminishes when the quantity used of that factor is increased, *ceteris paribus*.

In order to grow the potential of an economy, technological change is a particularly important factor because when the level of technology is higher the same amounts of input can create larger output. According to the Solow-Swan model, if productivity increases through technological progress then output per worker increases even when the economy is in the "steady state." What I mean by steady state here is that the economy is made up of a constant stock of physical wealth and a constant population size.

It isn't necessary that a country would be producing on its production possibilities frontier. Sometimes, due to inefficiencies, an economy doesn't use all its resources and produces inside its PPF.

As a result, there is a difference between the actual and potential output and this is known as the output gap. Lack of demand in an economy can cause unemployment of resources, this leads to a negative output gap. Similarly, there may be a positive output gap when the economy is producing beyond its production possibilities frontier. You might be wondering "what is she saying!? That's impossible." Well, it is possible because an economy goes through periodical trade cycles. There are fluctuations in the economic activity over a period of time. When the economy experiences a boom there is a positive output gap. It follows from here that an economy has an upturn, followed by a boom, followed by a downturn, and then followed by a recession. This cycle repeats itself over and over again.

Factors Affecting Economic Growth

As we just saw, an economy goes through the same trade cycle multiple times. In order to achieve economic growth that can be sustained over time, it is necessary for potential output to increase. This can be done in two ways: by increasing the quantity of resources or by increasing the quality of resources. Quantity of resources in an economy can be increased by increasing the country's population. This would mean that there would be more people to work and produce more output. Discovery of new resources such as new mines, or reclamation of land can increase the amount of resources that a country owns. The quality of human capital can be improved through education and training and better healthcare facilities. In order to improve the quality of capital goods, technological advances are necessary. When the quality of human resources is improved, more research and development follows.

DEVELOPED ECONOMY vs DEVELOPING ECONOMY

Measuring GDP

Measuring GDP is a crazy task. In any country, there are millions of firms and small businesses that produce output. There are three general methods to calculate the gross domestic product.

1. **Output method:** The output method measures the value of output produced by industries such as manufacturing, construction distribution, hotel and catering, and the agricultural sector. A problem with this method is that the same good can be counted twice. For example, a tire that is a part of a car might be counted twice if the output of the tire firm and the car firm both are counted.

2. **Income method:** The value of an outbreak produced is based on the cost involved in producing that output. These costs include wages, rents, interests, and profits. If all the payments to factors of production used in production are added up, the resulting figure would be the GDP of a country.

3. **The expenditure method:** What is produced in a year will either be sold or added to stocks. So, if additions to stock are added to expenditure on goods and services, a measure is obtained that will be equal to output and income. As I said before, one man's expenditure is another man's income.

Is GDP the Right Measure?

There are multiple problems with the GDP. First is that it is extremely difficult to have an accurate measure of the GDP. This is because of the existence of shadow economy. There are two main reasons why people may not declare their earned income. One is that they're seeking to evade paying tax, and the second is that the activity itself is illegal. Additionally, in countries with very low levels of literacy it is hard for the government to collect information about all economic activity. Some people may be unable to fill out the tax forms while others seek to evade them completely. The change in real GDP may not reflect the true change in the quantity of goods and services that households can enjoy if the level of undeclared economic activity changes over time. GDP per head does not give an accurate figure either because the population in different countries varies dramatically.

For instance, India has a population of over 1.3 billion people. This means that the GDP gets diluted over a way larger number of people. Conversely, Australia is under populated and the GDP is densely distributed.

Factors such as rate of crime, availability of consumer goods and services, leisure time, level of pollution, etc. have a great influence on the living standards of a country. Well, then, how are we supposed to compare the economic activity between different nations? There are multiple indicators that can be used. Let's dive in!

1. **Measurable Economic Welfare:** This measure was developed in 1972 by 2 American economists. The measure seeks to give a fuller picture of living standards by adjusting GDP figures to take into account other factors that have an impact on the standards of life. The indicator adds the value of GDP, leisure time, and unpaid work while the value of environmental damage is subtracted.

2. **Human Development Index:** The United Nations human development index takes into account the gross national income per head, educational attainment (as measured by mean years of schooling) and healthcare (measured by life expectancy). Countries with the highest human development index include Norway and the US, while countries with the lowest HDI are Niger and Central African Republic.

3. **Happiness Index:** Being happy in life is extremely important. This is why it is a great measure of standard of living of a country. The World Happiness Report is an annual publication of the United Nations Sustainable Development Solutions Network. It contains articles and rankings of national happiness based on respondent ratings of their own lives, [1] which the report also correlates with various life factors. Finland has been ranked first in this measure 3 years in a row.

Unemployment

People who are "unemployed" are basically jobless. Unemployment is defined by the US Bureau of Labor Statistics as people who do not have a job, have actively looked for work in the past four weeks, and currently are available for work. Also, people who were temporarily laid off and were waiting to be called back to that job are included in unemployment statistics. The labor force is all people who are of working age and able and willing to work. The key point is that the labor force includes both the employed and the unemployed.

Just like the market for goods and services, there is a market for labor. At the competitive market-clearing wage, every worker who wants a job can find one and the quantity of labor demanded is equal to the quantity of labor supplied. When the quantity demanded for labor is less than the quantity supplied, there is unemployment.

Types of Unemployment

1. Job Search and Frictional Unemployment

Frictional unemployment is the result of voluntary employment transitions within an economy. Frictional unemployment naturally occurs, even in a growing, stable economy.

It is always present in the economy and contributes to the overall employment picture and is part of natural unemployment, which is the minimum unemployment rate in an economy due to economic forces and movement of labor. The frictional unemployment rate is calculated by dividing the workers actively looking for jobs by the total labor force. Recent graduates from school and other first-time job seekers are included. Temporary transitions—such as moving to another town or city and workers quitting their job to look for better pay are also "frictionally unemployed." Unemployment benefits paid by the government can sometimes lead to frictional unemployment because the income allows workers to be selective in finding their next job, further adding to their time unemployed.

2. **Wage Rigidity and Structural Unemployment**

Structural unemployment occurs when the quantity supplied of labor persistently exceeds the quantity of labor demanded due to changes in the structure of an economy. This type of unemployment happens because though jobs are available, there's a mismatch between what companies need and what available workers offer. Technology tends to exacerbate structural unemployment, marginalizing certain workers, and rendering particular jobs, such as manufacturing, obsolete. It is a mismatch between the supply and demand for certain skills in the labor market.

For example, as old industries have declined, new industries have emerged, such as higher tech manufacture, IT, computing, insurance, and internet-based companies. However, these new industries may require a different skill set to previous manufacturing jobs, and it is this that can cause structural unemployment.

3. **Minimum Wage Laws**

This means that when minimum wages are applied, unemployment occurs as the OD<QS of labor. Economists refer to such people as involuntarily unemployed.

4. Labor Unions and Collective Bargaining

Collective bargaining refers to contract negotiations between firms and labor unions. A labor union is an organization of workers that advocated for better working conditions, pay, and benefits for its members (by threatening to strike).

Collective bargaining generally leads to equilibrium wages and benefits that are greater than what workers would have received under market-clearing wage. Hence, OD<QS of labor.

5. Efficiency Wages

The idea of the efficiency wage theory is that increasing wages can lead to increased labor productivity because workers feel more motivated to work with higher pay.

Efficiency wages are wages above the lowest pay that workers would accept: employers use them to increase motivation and productivity. For example, in 1914, Henry Ford increased the daily wage from $2.34 to $5.00. Doubling the average wage helped ensure a stable workforce and likely boosted sales since the workers could now afford to buy the cars they were making.

NEED TO LEARN HOW TO CODE ASAP OR ILL GET FIRED TOMORROW! UGH!

6. **Downward Wage Rigidity**

   Downward wage rigidity occurs when workers resist a cut in their wages. Cuts in wages hurt worker morale and lower productivity. As a result, many firms would fire people instead of cutting their wages. Downward wage rigidity, like the other forms of wage rigidity, tends to keep the wages remain above the market-clearing wage.

7. **Cyclical Unemployment and the Natural Rate of Unemployment**

   Cyclical unemployment is the impact of economic recession or expansion on the total unemployment rate. Cyclical unemployment relates to the irregular ups and downs, or cyclical trends in growth and production, as measured by the gross domestic product (GDP) that occur within the business cycle. Most business cycles eventually reverse, with the downturn shifting to an upturn, followed by another downturn. Economists describe cyclical unemployment as the result of businesses not having enough demand for labor to employ all those who are looking for work at that point within the business cycle. When demand for a product and service declines, there can be a corresponding reduction in supply production to compensate. As the supply levels are reduced, fewer employees are required to meet the lower standard of production volume. Those workers who are no longer needed will be released by the company, resulting in their unemployment

   When economic output falls, the business cycle is low and cyclical unemployment will rise. Conversely, when business cycles are at their peak, cyclical unemployment will tend to be low because there is high demand for labor.

   Unfortunately, cyclical unemployment can become a self-fueling downward spiral. The newly unemployed have less disposable income, lowering demand and business revenue, thus leading to even more layoffs. Without intervention, this spiral continues until supply has dropped to meet the lowered demand. Unfortunately, this may not happen until unemployment reaches 25%. This height of unemployment is what happened during the Great Depression, which lasted a decade. While monetary policies were implemented at the time, it was not enough. It is generally accepted that what truly ended the Depression was the demand for military equipment and supplies as the United States entered World War II. The highest rate of US unemployment was 24.9% in 1933, during the Great Depression. Unemployment remained above 14% from 1931 to 1940. It remained in the single digits until September 1982 when it reached 10.1%. During the Great Recession, unemployment reached 10% in October 2009.

4. **Voluntary Unemployment**

Voluntary unemployment refers to the situation when the worker deliberately chooses not to work because of a low wage scale or not able to find out suitable employment for him.

The voluntary unemployment also gets created when the worker is neither willing to work nor searches for a job, as he is satisfied with the amount given by the government in the form of unemployment benefits. High-income tax rates could also be one of the reasons behind a worker not choosing to work.

5. **Seasonal Unemployment**

Seasonal unemployment occurs when people are unemployed at particular times of the year when demand for labor is lower than usual. For example, in a ski resort, unemployment is likely to be higher in the summer when there is no snow. Often, unemployment falls around Christmas time because extra jobs are available (e.g., Royal Mail taking on extra workers for mail delivery).

In tourist areas, seasonal unemployment could be a big problem because work is only available for a few months a year.

Because of seasonal unemployment, official government statistics on unemployment are often seasonally adjusted. This means the rate of unemployment is adjusted to take into account the usual seasonal fluctuations.

6. Disguised Unemployment

Disguised unemployment is a kind of unemployment in which there are people who are visibly employed but are actually unemployed. This situation is also known as 'hidden unemployment.' In such a situation, more people are engaged in a work than required. For example:

1. In rural areas, this type of unemployment is generally found in the agricultural sector, like in a family of 9 people all are engaged in the same agricultural plot. But if 4 people are withdrawn from it there will be no reduction in output. So, these 4 people are actually facing disguised unemployment.

IM TRANSITIONING BETWEEN JOBS

I DONT HAVE WORK TO DO IN THE WINTERS!

OOP! I HATE TO WORK, ILL SPEND DAD'S MONEY

FRICTIONAL UNEMPLOYMENT

SEASONAL UNEMPLOYMENT

VOLUNTARY UNEMPLOYMENT

2. In urban areas, this type of unemployment can be seen mostly in service sectors such as in a family where all members are engaged in one petty shop or a small business which can be managed by less number of persons.

7. **Casual Unemployment**

Casual Unemployment is when the worker is employed on a day-to-day basis for a contractual job and has to leave it once the contract terminates. Simply, the inevitable time delay when a worker transits from one job to another due to the expiration of a previous job contract is called as casual unemployment.

Casual unemployment is prevalent in industries which work on contract basis such as building construction, agriculture, etc. where the workers are hired on a day-to-day basis and leave the company on the accomplishment of the work.

The workers who are released after the termination of a contract are included in the list of casual unemployed workers, and they are considered unemployed until they find suitable jobs elsewhere or renew the contract.

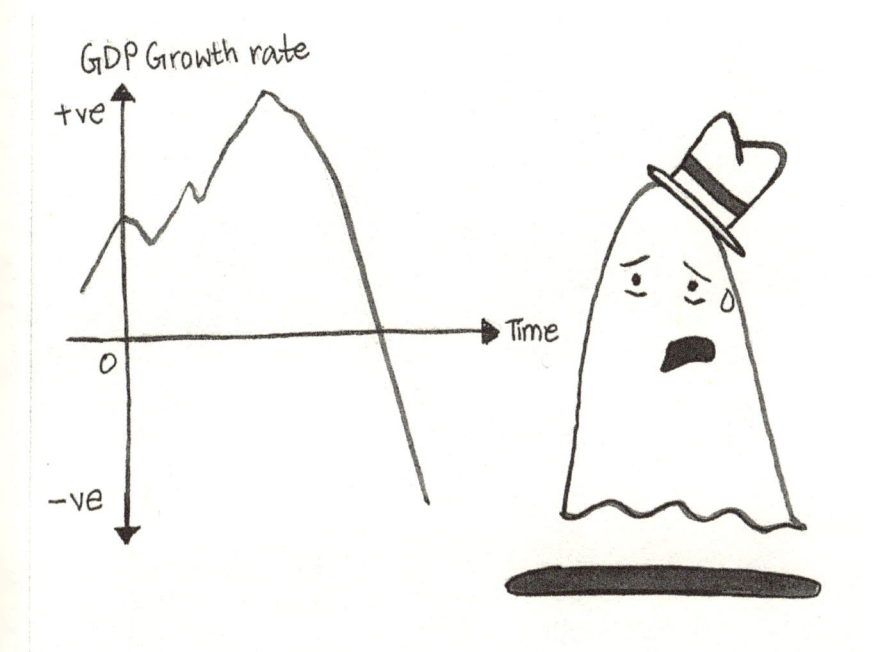

Chapter - 7
COUNTERCYCLICAL ECONOMIC POLICY

Chapter 7
COUNTERCYCLICAL ECONOMIC POLICIES

As we saw before, an economy is really moody. It has its ups and downs. The government, in this context, is the therapist. In order to correct the fluctuations and bring the economy to a sort of "equilibrium" position, they use counter cyclical monetary and fiscal policies. The main instruments used here are taxation, government expenditure, money supply, and interest rates. In this segment, will be looking at these in detail.

Monetary Policy

Counter cyclical monetary policy is conducted by the Central Bank. For example, it is the Federal Reserve Bank in the US (also known as the Fed), the RBI in India, and so on. They achieve this by manipulating interest rates and bank reserves. If the economy is contracting, the Central Bank would want to use expansionary monetary policies. Similarly, if the economy is expanding at an uncontrollable rate, then the Central Bank would use contractionary monetary policies.

When the Central Bank reduces the interest in an economy, the long-term interest rates also fall. If the interest rate is low, the reward for saving would be less. Naturally, people would rather consume or invest in business. If business boom and consumption rises, more goods would be demanded. This would require more people to work and unemployment rates would also fall. This is the expansionary monetary policy. The opposite happens in contractionary monetary policy. The Central Bank increases the short term interest rates and reduces the access to credit. Since the reward for saving is to hire, more people put their money in savings accounts and spend less. The aggregate demand in the economy falls, more people become unemployed, and the economy contracts.

Other tools that the Central Bank can use are the reserve requirement, interest paid on reserves deposits, lending from the discount window, and quantitative easing.

If the Central Bank decreases the quantity of required reserves, the private banks demand for reserves decreases. This leads to a fall in the long-term interest rate in an economy. The Central Bank can also decrease the quantity of required reserves by private banks by reducing the interest rate paid on reserves. This is another way of carrying out an expansionary monetary policy.

Quantitative easing is a very important tool that the Central Bank uses. It indulges in open market operations. Purchasing long-term bonds in an open market operation reduces their supply. This decreases their price, and hence, the long-term interest rates fall. The opposite happens when the Central Bank sells away those bonds.

Fiscal Policy

Countercyclical fiscal policy is passed by the legislative part of the government. They manage the fluctuations through changing the rate of tax and the amount of government expenditure.

The fiscal policy can be divided into automatic and discretionary components. Automatic stabilizers are those components of the government budget that automatically adjust to smooth out economic fluctuations. Tax is one such example. If an economy is in a recession, less people are employed. Since less people have money, the revenue from income tax automatically decreases.

Discretionary components are those aspects of the government's fiscal policy that the policymakers deliberately enact in order to nullify the economic fluctuations. This mostly involves government spending on various schemes.

If the economy is under a recession, the government will try to expand economy through expansionary fiscal policy. It would cut taxes and increase government spending on things such as welfare and unemployment benefits. Since the taxes are lowered, people would have more money in their pockets. They would spend this money on consumer goods, which would increase the demand for goods in general. More would be produced and demand for labor would also increase. The economy would then flourish. If there's very high inflation and the economy is getting out of hand, the government uses contractionary fiscal policies. Here, they would increase tax rates and decrease government spending. People would have less money and would demand less goods. The lower demand would put a downward pressure on the prices in the economy and inflation would decrease.

These countercyclical policies only work in the short run. They must be used wisely otherwise the government could create hyper inflation or have a huge debt. There is also an opportunity cost involved with employing these countercyclical policies. The resources spent on connecting these could have been spent on better things such as education, sanitation, and infrastructure. The money could also have been used for paying off national debts.

Supply Side Policies

If the government wishes to improve a country's economic performance in the long run, they must employ supply side policies. Supply side policies include programs that are intended to improve literacy rates, healthcare facilities, infrastructure development, and more. The government must also invest in research and development to have better technology that would increase the total product of an economy even in the steady state.

Supply side policies have 2 broad categories. Free-market supply side policies and interventionist supply side policies. Free-market supply side policies aim to increase the amount of competition in an economy. As we saw earlier, greater competition leads to a larger quantity of output and better quality products. The government promotes privatization and deregulates the market to a larger extent. Tax cuts, removal of the "red tape", more flexible labor markets, and free trade agreements are some features of free supply side policy measures. Interventionist supply side policies promote nationalization. There are more state-owned enterprises, government-funded education, government medicare schemes, and housing when there is more government intervention.

The overall aim is to create economic growth in the long run. However, there are pros and cons associated with both these schemes.

Nationalization vs. Privatization

Nationalization

Nationalization is the process of transforming privately-owned assets into public assets by bringing them under the public ownership of a national government or state. Nationalization often happens in developing countries and can reflect a nation's desire to control assets or to assert its dominance over foreign-owned industries. Often, the companies or assets are taken over and little to no compensation is provided to the previous owners.

Nationalization might benefit an economy by the production of more merit goods and fewer demerit goods. This would cause positive externalities in the economy. More free goods such as street lights will also be produced. However, nationalization removes the element of competition and incentive to profit.

Efficiency is, hence, lower in state-owned enterprises as compared to private companies.

In India, the airlines "Air India" was nationalized under the Air Corporations Act 1953. Following this, in 1969, 14 banks were nationalized. The coal industry under Coal India Limited and the oil and gas industry under the Oil and Natural Gas Corporation were also nationalized in India.

Privatization

Privatization occurs when a government-owned business, operation, or property becomes owned by a private, non-government party. It helps governments save money and increase efficiency. It is believed that privatization leads to greater efficiency in the market because manufacturers have the incentive of profit. Wasteful spending is also dramatically decreased. The "bureaucratic red tape," which is prominent in government-owned enterprises, can also be avoided. Note that privatization also describes the transition of a company from being publicly traded to becoming privately held. This is referred to as corporate privatization. However, necessities like electricity, water, and schools shouldn't be vulnerable to market forces or driven by profit. If left to the market forces, public and free goods would be highly under produced and a large amount of demerit goods would be produced. This would lead to negative externalities in the market. Moreover, if a firm gains too much power and becomes a monopoly, it could potentially exploit consumers. Brand loyalty can also threaten consumer sovereignty.

EPILOGUE

Through Nero's journey of growing his business, a ghost emoji like Keynes, and with all the ups and downs in the "Ghost world", I hope you could learn something about basic Economics. But it does not end here! This is where the interesting bit begins.

You can dive into other specific areas of Economics such as Behavioral, Development, Mathematical and more. Having knowledge of Economics is as important as having knowledge of any other Science or Social Science. The basic concept of scarcity makes one realize the importance of protecting the resources of planet; the importance of time and in some cases, the importance of opportunity.

I am thrilled that you have already taken the first step towards learning Economics, and hope that you would light heartedly (if not as a straight up PhD!) include its lessons in your daily life.

Made in the USA
Coppell, TX
23 June 2021